UNDERSTANDING
CAUSALITY

Also by Jean Piaget

The Child's Conception of Number
Genetic Epistemology
The Origins of Intelligence in Children
Play, Dreams and Imitation in Childhood

with Bärbel Inhelder

The Child's Conception of Space
The Early Growth of Logic in the Child

☐ JEAN PIAGET

with the collaboration of R. Garcia

UNDERSTANDING CAUSALITY

Translated by Donald and Marguerite Miles

W · W · NORTON & COMPANY · INC · NEW YORK

Translation Copyright © 1974 by W. W. Norton & Company, Inc.
Originally published as *Les Explications Causales*
© 1971, *Presses Universitaires de France*
ISBN 0 393 01110 0

Published simultaneously in Canada
by George J. McLeod Limited, Toronto
Library of Congress Cataloging in Publication Data
Piaget, Jean, 1896–
  Understanding causality.
  Translation of Les explications causales.
  1. Causation. I. Garcia, R. II. Title.
BD542.P513 1974   122   73–22414
ISBN 0–393–01110–0

This book was designed by Robert Freese.
Typefaces used are Perpetua and Times Roman.
Manufacturing was done by Vail-Ballou Press.

Printed in the United States of America

1 2 3 4 5 6 7 8 9 0

Contents

Foreword

During the past few years, the research of the International Center for Genetic Epistemology has dealt with causality, in its broadest sense, including every explanation of a material phenomenon, both the physical aspects of actions and their relationships to objects. The stages in the development of the understanding of causality pose much more difficult problems than the study of operations of the subjects. Because operations essentially show the general coordinations of the action, the stages of their formulation conform to an inner logic that analysis sooner or later succeeds in drawing out, and that is found again with rather striking regularity in the most diverse fields. Explaining a physical phenomenon must presume the use of such operations because the search for causality always ends up in going beyond the observable and in having recourse to inferred, therefore operational connections. But, in addition, there are the responses of the object, which are of critical importance, because to talk of causality is to presume that objects exist outside of us and that they act independently of us. If the causal model adopted includes an inferential part, the explanation of the phenomenon has the sole purpose of identifying the properties of the object. These properties can resist as well as yield to the subject's operational treatment, resulting in the development of explanations that do not necessarily present the same regularity nor the same relative simplicity as that of logico-mathematical operations.

Consequently, as we began to doubt the existence of stages in this evolution, we had to undertake a much greater number of research studies than anticipated, so diverse were the fields to be explored. Furthermore, each new analysis threatened to contradict as well as complete some of the preceding ones since, let us repeat, the causal explanation depends more on the objects than on the subjects. It would therefore have been rash for us to publish our first results before reaching a certain degree of certainty. We now find ourselves in the following situation: We are in possession of about a hundred studies, completed and written up, which we expect to divide into separate small books bearing on the essential points of causal explanation: transmission of movements, problems of directions, composition of forces, sufficient reason, states of matter, exchange of heat, etc. However, our concern is that, in being presented with these separate studies, the reader will fail to grasp both the guiding hypotheses and the overall results.

This introduction has been written to remedy this state of affairs. In no way does it pretend to replace detailed analysis because, in such fields, only these facts count that have been sufficiently researched to justify their interpretations. On the other hand, by summarizing in broad outline the accumulated data, this foreword will define precisely the main problems that these data pose and indicate in which direction the solutions may lie. Once in possession of these guidelines, the reader can more easily understand the later *Studies,* with each section then being complete in itself as well as fitting into the general picture.

Actually, the hypotheses stemming from these facts turn out to be very simple. E. Meyerson saw in causality a product of *a priori* reasoning, putting an identification by reason in conflict with a variable and irrational reality, and P. Frank admits to having hesitated, throughout his career, to look upon causality as a law of nature or a tautological inference. On the contrary, however, the psychogenesis of causal explanations seems to us to show that these explanations bear as much on transformations of objects as on transmissions or conservations, while the operations of the subject intervening in the play of inferences can be an agent of transformation as well as of conservation. The result is a progressive convergence of operations and causality, the former stemming from the subject and the latter from the object. This convergence appears as a system of operations, attributed only to objects and set in reality, showing what happens when these objects react on each other and behave like operators.

Consequently, a new problem emerges. Since the subject himself constitutes, by his actions as well as by his organism, a source of causality linked with reality, must we conclude that his own operations stem from this causality? Or must we conclude that the operational structures resulting from the general coordinates of the action constitute in their logico-mathematical aspects the necessary forms of all knowledge, including that of causal relationships? In other words, must the notion of the attribution of operations to objects be interpreted in a realistic or an *a prioristic* manner? Since the essential aim of genetic studies is to discover continual dialectic processes in development itself, we could be tempted to answer at the outset that it is neither one nor the other, nor the two together, nor yet one after the other like a spiral. But, since, according to our methods, we are suspicious of speculations and rely mainly on facts, we shall limit ourselves in the present essay to providing for each stage the experimental data that would best seem to cover the topic. As for the sequence of our studies, it is obviously in the area of the action itself and of its two dimensions, the causal and the operational, that the elements of a positive answer will be found. This is the direction that we have taken starting with this year's work.

While awaiting these new results, the present essay includes two parts. In the first, which constitutes the main part of the book, the principal data furnished by those studies already completed will be summed up, with the details to be published at a later date. However, this summary will be presented in the general perspective of the relationships between causality and operations, since this seems to be the main question raised by causal explanations. The second part, written by R. Garcia and the author, is a discussion of the problem of relationships between geometry and dynamics as it arises in modern physics and, in a renewed form, in contemporary physics, which at the same time constitutes an essential aspect of the general question of causality, starting with the elementary stages of psychogenesis.

Finally, we provide two kinds of guidelines for reading the following pages. First, we shall not give the title of each research report nor the name of the respective collaborators along with the quotations. A complete list of these reports will be found in the bibliography at the end of Part One, and references to them will be made simply with the notations R1, R2, etc. . . .

Second, we shall refer each fact mentioned back to one of the stages observed in the course of the development of causality. These stages correspond generally to those of operations. Here, then, is the series:

Level IA (age 4 to 5)	Preoperational reactions prior to the formation of constituting functions (volume XXII of *Studies*).
Level IB (age 5 1/2 to 6)	Beginnings of objectivization and constituting functions.
Level IIA (age 7 to 8)	Formation of concrete operations (classes, relations, numbers, and spaces) and of the first conservations; transitivity.
Level IIB (age 9 to 10)	Completion of concrete operations; conservation of weight during the process of changes of forms of the object; natural coordinates of space.
Level IIIA (age 11 to 12)	Propositional operations, combinatorial analysis, group of the two reversibilities, possible coordination of two systems of references.
Level IIIB (age 12 to 15)	Equilibration and generalization of the IIIA reactions.

In closing, I wish to express my thanks to the numerous collaborators at the Center whose names will be found in the listing of the hundred studies used and briefly summarized in this book, as well as to my colleagues, F. Halbwachs, J. B. Grize, P. Gréco, and R. Garcia, who were kind enough to read the manuscript and whose advice and suggestions have been most valuable.

J. PIAGET

PART ONE

Causality and Operations

by Jean Piaget

Explaining a phenomenon by means of a set of conditions considered as causal amounts to showing, on the one hand, through what transformations it was produced and, on the other, how the new aspects of the result correspond to certain transmissions from the initial stages. This dual aspect of production and conservation is characteristic of operational as well as causal transformations, and is evident in both by the fact that the construction in question seems neccessary. Seen genetically, the operations transform the real and thus correspond to what the subject can do to the objects in his deductive or deductible manipulations, which are at first material but susceptible of progressively formal refinement. Causality, on the other hand, expresses what the objects do as they act on one another and on the subject. There must, therefore, be an intimate relationship between these two kinds of actions; otherwise the logico-mathematical constructions of the subject would never meet with reality, while reality would modify the subject's operations without his knowing it.

1. The Possible Primacy of Operations

Three kinds of relationships are therefore possible, and a choice must be made among them. According to the first, the logico-mathematical operations of the subject would develop on their own by reflexive abstractions starting with the general coordinations of his actions. With the progression of this endogenous construction, the operational instruments, newly fashioned, step by step, would in turn be attributed to the objects, which would lead to the formation of new kinds of explanation, and therefore new causal structures. As we begin to study the subject's operations, while neglecting more or less the particulars of the problems of causality, this is what apparently happens. For example, when the child attains the level of operational transitivity, he arrives at the notions of the mediate transmission of motion. When he succeeds in coordinating two systems of reference, he acquires at the same time the power to master certain vectorial problems, and so on. In short, in this first approach, the operations would develop through their own means, and causality would consist only of a kind of response or series of successive responses of the operational structures gradually acquired. In this case the notion of attributing the operation to the objects would take on a significance approaching a kind of *a priorism,* definitely genetic or evolutive and certainly not static, but with more emphasis on the role of the subject than on that of the objects.

However, such an interpretation raises two kinds of objections, some from the point of view of causality and others from that of the operations themselves. Beginning with the operations, it is evident that the more elementary and the more *a fortiori* they are, the further we go back toward their preoperational roots (functions, etc.) and the less they are dissociated from their substance, which then depends on the object and only indirectly on causality. The big difference, for example, between the "concrete" operations of the 7- to 11-year-old and later formal or propositional operations is that they bear directly on the objects and thus are partially inseparable from their contents. This results in time lags, as in the case of conservations, seriations, transitivities, and so on, applicable to weight, with only one or two years' delay in the case of simple quantities. This resistance of content to form and, in other instances, the help provided by contents that are easily structured operationally, cannot be separated from the factors of causality. It seems evident, in the instance of weight, that the difficulties of dynamic interpretation presented by this notion play a big role in the delay of its operational structuration, because of the contradictions that must be overcome between the demands of the structuration and the diversity of objective causal situations. The same applies to volume, the delayed logicalization of which seems to be linked to geometric problems of internal continuum (the parts taken as a whole), and, in the case of the volume of the body, to corpuscular physical models—both kinds of considerations going beyond the realm of concrete operations.

Generally, these concrete operations present themselves in two forms, which are isomorphic although distinct, the respective psychogenetic developments of both being closely bound together. These two forms are logical operations bearing on objects that are discontinuous in terms of their likenesses and differences, and the infralogical operations bearing on the spatial continuum in terms of proximities and separations. Space, because of its dual logico-mathematical and physical nature, is one of the closest points of contact between subject and objects, the spatial operations playing a fundamental role in the development of causality. It is therefore very likely that causality plays an important role in the evolution of operations.

As for the preoperational structures, let us remember that they are characterized by a lack of differentiation between the spatial and the logico-arithmetic, as opposed to the differentiations and coordinations characteristic of concrete operations (figural collections and figural numbers are examples of the latter). These prelogical forms of classification, and so on, are very closely linked to a causal or precausal content (definitions through usage, figural collections based on functional relations, etc.). On the other hand, the constituent functions that develop at the same levels, and that represent the semilogic peculiar to these structures, express the physical dependencies leading to causality as well as the conceptual dependencies leading to the operations of the subject. Obviously the conceptual dependencies, like the physical dependencies, are rooted in the action itself, in its fundamental sensori-motor components. The subject's operations take their form from general coordinations while causality draws part of its information from specific actions, but it is clear that between these specific actions and the general coordinations there exist close ties, and their differentiation remains very gradual.

For all these reasons, it is therefore unlikely that the development of operations is independent of the development of causality and that it determines its course of action. Conversely, the hypothesis of a simple subordination of the causal to the operational encounters considerable difficulties from the point of view of causality itself. Indeed, there exists a remarkable convergence between the stages of formation of the operations and those of causal explanation; the subject understands the phenomenon only by attributing to objects first actions and then operations more or less isomorphic to his. But this does not mean that these operations were performed independently of causality. From the standpoint of causality, the problem can be identified as follows: Why do certain forms of explanation appear simpler than others, and why do they precede them in history and in individual development? For example, the notions of mechanical thrust or pull seem more elementary than those of heat or electromagnetism, but actually, the phenomena of thrust and pull do not occur anymore often than the others. To say that they are more primitive because they stem from simpler operations only shifts the problem, since we have yet to explain why they appear so to us. To say that these operations, like the mechanical explanations, are simple, to the degree that they both proceed from actions or from coordinations imposed from the beginning of the development by the structure of our organism, puts us on the right track, but then shows us immediately that the relationships between the *schèmes* * leading to operations and those that, from the outset, present a causal significance are much more complex than a direct descendance.

In fact, if we assume that operations can be derived from some aspects characteristic of the preceding material actions, we immediately place ourselves on causal grounds. Assembling objects into collections presupposing classes, putting them in order presupposing seriations, or even relating them according to different arrangements before such actions are internalized into purely mental or deductive operations, still amounts to acting on objects and therefore to displacing them, pushing them, putting them in stable positions, etc. Therefore we have, from the outset, a whole causal context, from which the operations are formed. If it later becomes easy to abstract from this dynamism speeds, durations, and even spatial configurations in order to arrive at extratemporal and extraphysical forms—not necessarily metaphysical, as for example infinite arithmetic—we must not forget that the independence of the operational from the causal is a product of refinement and not a basic datum. When, finally, the same operations are used by the subject to understand transitive motion and kinematic and dynamic transmissions, for example, we can certainly speak of an "attribution" of these operations to objects, but on the condition that we do not forget that during their formation the subject himself was, according to his own organism, one object among others, subject to all sorts of dependencies and physical interactions in the specific actions by means of which he has manipulated or transformed objects. Moreover, we should keep in mind that the subject, however young he may be, becomes conscious of these aids or resistances to reality at the same time as he becomes conscious of his power over objects so that, for him as for the observer who follows his development, causality is as primitive as the formative "schèmes" of future operations.

* *Translator's note:* "Whatever is repeatable and generalizable in an action is what I have called a 'schème' . . ." Jean Piaget, *Genetic Epistemology,* Norton, New York, 1970, p. 42.

2. The Primacy of Causality

Let us examine, then, the inverse hypothesis: Causality precedes the operation or the preoperational actions, and the development of these operations constitutes a reflection, first internalized and then formalized, of the causal notions successively imposed on the subject by reality. Actually, leaving aside the general tendencies of empiricist epistemology, such an interpretation is not lacking for arguments. Starting with the most general, if operations are born of actions and if their function is like that of actions, that is, to transform reality, it seems obvious that the subject will try to transform it materially, and therefore causally, before indulging in formal transformations by enriching it with classifications, seriations, enumerations, measures, etc. Briefly, we could maintain that, before structuring objects, the subject will try to utilize them, and therefore to modify them with an eye toward effects or physical modifications, which implies an indefinite whole of causal interactions. In such a perspective, each operational progress rises from a need for comprehension that is initially triggered by a problem of causality, which must be "explained" forthwith. In order to do this, a number of real or apparent contradictions must first be eliminated. Many examples can be interpreted this way. If we must wait for the average age of 9 for an understanding of the conservation of lengths, the construction of systems of coordinations, etc., without going back to the conservation of weight, it is quite possible that this operational progress is closely linked to the noticeable transformations that occur at this age in the child's explanations of dynamics.[1] Although up to this time the motions and speeds (impulse [*élans*], etc.) were forces in themselves, we now observe a differentiation between kinematics and the play of forces, which imposes new precisions when it comes to paths taken, to positions and orientations in space, etc. Weight, therefore, plays, among other things, a new role, and the horizontality of water, which is a particular case of the application of natural coordinates, is at once geometrically discovered and causally explained by the weight of

[1] See the end of § 8.

liquid, until then considered light, and by its tendency to flow downwards. In short, a great many facts can be invoked in favor of the role of causality in the conquest of operational structuration.

However, this kind of presentation presents difficulties as great as those in the preceding hypothesis. The main difficulty is that, in considering the development of causal explanations as preceding that of operations or as being independent of them, it is necessary to interpret causality as being due to either the experience of objects or to the actions themselves, but only as physical experiences rooted in the interactions between the organism and the objects. In fact, to have recourse to the general coordinations of the action is already to invoke the formative structures of future operations since, to combine actions, to fit them together, to put them in order, and to relate them already implies a prelogical or premathematical structuration. So, explaining causality independently of operations amounts to considering causal relationships as data directly observable in the immediate experience of the objects or of the actions, and capable of being deduced from them by simple or physical abstraction, as opposed to reflexive or logico-mathematical abstraction, without recourse to either a construction or a composition.

Hume has definitively proved that, in adhering to this method of simple empirical reading with abstraction from objects alone, we end up not with causality but with purely regular successions of laws. It is true that Michotte has since demonstrated the existence of a perception of causality, the pertinence of which anyone can verify, but we have then tried to identify precisely two points that are essential to our present discussion. The first is that this perception bears on the resultant of a composition. As Michotte himself admits, we see nothing passing from an active *A* mobile to a passive *B* mobile. We do see an "effect" dependent on speeds, durations, and displacements. We shall add, then, that this impression of production results from an elementary composition according to which, in the course of transformation, what *B* gained corresponds to what *A* lost. If operations are still not involved, there is at least a preoperational construction by perceptive or sensori-motor regulations, and not a perception of an actual transmission. We notice that "something has passed"—and not that something "is passing" from *A* to *B*, which is very different. These perceptive impressions would also be unexplainable if they did not come from a displacement in terms of visual indices, from tactilo-kinesthetic perceptions linked to the sensori-motor action itself. This leads us back to the action.

Effectively, starting with the sensori-motor level, we witness the formation of a causality linked to the actions of moving, pushing, pulling, balancing, etc., and therefore we can see in it a whole development prior to that of operations. But the whole problem consists once again in establishing whether this development is the product of simple observations, as though the causal relation had been observed in the form of a displacement or a change of light, or whether it is already a matter of construction or composition. The whole development of sensori-motor causality in the direction of objectivization and spatialization shows that it is interdependent with the constructions of the object in space and time—in other words, of the entire intelligence. On the other hand, from the first causal behavior of pushing, pulling, etc., these actions constitute products of composition starting with prehension and spatial relationships. It is enough to say that in every sensori-motor causality we find at work the system of *schèmes* of intelligence and their general coordinations, which is the first form of what will later constitute operations.

3. Interaction Between Operational Compositions and Causality

Our hypothesis will be that at every level the development of the understanding of causality proceeds by interacting with the development of the operations, which amounts to saying that each of these two developments helps the other, following conflicts as well as convergences, so that we can never speak of a one-way action except on special and momentary occasions and in alternating successions. But a number of problems present themselves, which we shall only state here and discuss later.

The first of these questions is the progressive differentiation of the two present systems. When the subject verifies the commutation of a numerical addition, we see in this behavior a noncausal operation, while if he tries to understand why two pendulums that are set in motion, facing each other, exchange their initial positions, we speak of causality. But if the first of these operations is not yet symbolically or deductively executed, and if the subject needs to manipulate objects to control or even understand commutation—for example, that $2 + 3 = 3 + 2$—the actions he carries out are at the same time both operational, or preoperational, and causal, since he shifts objects and since a dynamic process intervenes between his hands and these objects. However, the subject's intention is not to try to analyze it. He can neglect this mechanical aspect in order to focus on his problem of commutation, especially since the causal action of displacing objects has become familiar to him, and an explanation would have no influence on his comprehension of the commutative relationships. On the contrary, at the sensori-motor level, when a baby experiments with displacements of objects, he will try to change AB into BA, but his whole effort will be concentrated on the movements necessary to this change of position. The emphasis will then be on the problems of causality, although this will not prevent him from recognizing that it is still the same objects A and B—and that is the beginning of commutation.

Since causality proceeds from a specific action to a generalization of relationships between objects and, since the operations themselves are derived from actions and from their coordinations, we can assume that the further back one goes, the more the actions of the subject are undifferentiated, therefore simultaneously preoperational and causal; as the operations progress, there will be at the same time differentiation and collaboration in a manner yet to be determined. Given these continuous interactions, the first problem is to state precisely the criteria we shall use:

(a) The logico-algebraic operations of the subject consist of transforming concrete or abstract objects by enriching them with new forms such as classes, order, correspondences, morphisms, etc., the construction of which proceeds by reflexive abstractions starting with operations of a lower order or general coordinations of action.

(b) Geometric operations proceed likewise, but by construction of forms that may already belong to the object (physical space). From this comes the possibility of reflexive abstractions, permitting the construction of new forms, capable on a higher level of going beyond reality, and of "simple" or physical abstractions, starting with the spatio-temporal structures of objects.

(c) As soon as their relationships can be repeated, facts and laws bear on the observable properties of objects and their variations which are all discovered by simple abstractions, beginning with objects. On the other hand, the very reading of these facts assumes the use of instruments of assimilation, such as classes, relationships, measures, etc., the formation of which is derived from reflexive abstraction. *A fortiori,* the same holds true when isolated variations become, when connected together, covariations or functional dependent variables, the function $y = f(x)$ being an "application" that also supposes a coordinative activity of the subject, even if the variations of x and y are discovered by physical or simple abstraction.

(d) Causality consists of a system of transformations, which are not directly observable, that account for the variations (c) by a deductive process analogous to the operational construction (a) but resulting in the construction of a model attributed to objects. Causality, like geometric constructions and functions, therefore includes a mixture of simple abstractions furnishing the data and reflexive abstractions intervening in the construction of the model.

(e) The causal actions of the subject on objects, or those of which the subject is the center, do not give rise to direct, or distorting, intuitions. They are known only because of active controls leading to the knowledge of covariations in terms of results observed on the objects,[1] and thus they require a deductive construction analogous to (d). These causal actions are therefore known by analogy with the causality between objects, just as causality is known by analogy with the operations of the subject.

Consequently, two essential distinctions must be made. As far as operations (a) are concerned, we can speak of specific opera-

[1] For example, the control of the actions of thrust and the directing of instruments in opposition to sight when only the direction of the eye is actively regulated, the physiological adjustments remaining subconscious.

tions, as in the case of a grouping of classes, $A + A' = B$, or a dissociation, $B - A' = A$, etc. But we must also consider the transformations of one operation into another—such as inversion, reciprocity, or correlativity—in the group INRC, including as well in this category the general forms of composition—such as transitivity, associativity, and distributivity.

In the second place, when, in order to discover the facts and laws (c), the subject needs operations as instruments of reading and structuration, we shall speak of operations "applied to the object." These operations include not only the elementary establishment of relationships or measures, but also the vast sum of functions used by the physicist to express the laws in his field of study. On the other hand, in the construction of a causal model starting with the qualitative forms of transmission understood by the child and proceeding to the structures of groups and of operators used by the physicist, the operations in question become explainable only when they can be "attributed" to objects, since it is necessary to understand the actions of these objects. We shall see that these attributed operations consist less of specific operations than of transformations of operations just referred to, therefore, in general, of forms of operational composition.[2] We shall therefore have to determine whether the operational progress of these attributed operations acts only on that of causality, or whether and in what way there is an interaction.

4. Mediate Transmissions and Transitivity

One of the most common cases of convergence between a general form of operational composition and a process invoked in a causal explanation is that of the semi-internal, mediate transmission of movements, etc., which develops at about age 7 to 8, at a level where operational transitivity begins. Indeed, opera-

---

[2] To avoid any equivocation, however, let us specify at once that in attributing an operational transformation to objects, the subject is obliged to apply it to his own use. There is therefore nothing contradictory in its being simultaneously applied and attributed.

tional transitivity constitutes one of the conditions necessary for the construction of groupings of concrete operations. The equivalences (symmetrical relationships), the seriations, the nestings [*emboîtements*] of classes and correspondences, all presuppose this transitivity, which is an indispensable instrument of mediate inferences. At the same time, we see a general pattern of composition of similar nature appearing in the realm of causality.

From the sensori-motor beginnings of causality, the subject discovers all kinds of transmissions, since the simplest causal relationship between an agent and a recipient of the action presupposes the transmission of something—movement, force, etc. As soon as he tries to displace, push, or pull an object, a baby learns to understand such transmissions. This is shown in the data of R1, where we examined how young subjects estimate the resistance when an active ball *A* at the foot of a slope sets in motion a passive ball *B*, or a cart whose weight we can vary. From age 5½ onwards, half of the subjects, and a few from age 4, expect that an increase in the weight of *B* will reduce the effect of the thrust, while for the others, it will increase it.

But we must wait until age 7 to 8 before the notion of a mediate transmission is added to these immediate transmissions, that is, through immobile mediating objects, and the problem is to understand what factors are at work. R2 deals with intermediaries formed by a row of marbles, the last of which starts rolling after the first has been hit by an active marble. At level IA (age 4 to 5), the active marble is expected to act at a distance, without intermediaries involved, or to go behind the others in order to push the last one—or even to take its place! At level IB (age 6), the transmission of the movement is understood as a chain reaction of immediate transmissions. The first one touched pushes the second one, etc., with a general movement and without anything going through the marbles. In stage II, on the other hand, there is a mediate transmission but in a semi-internal form, the impetus [*élan*], etc., passing through the marbles, and a semi-external one with the marbles moving forward just a little. It is only in stage III that the mediate transmission becomes purely internal, that is without molar translation, but with an internal jolt, "vibrations," etc.

R3 verified these results by utilizing as intermediaries obviously immobile objects: a glass held upside down and pushed into artificial moss, two coins pressed down by two fingers, etc. Despite these precautions the subjects of stage II continue to believe in little displacements without which transmission seems to them to be impossible, and once again we must wait until stage III for a purely internal mediation.

R4 deals with two transmissions coming from opposite directions, an active marble hitting a row of immobile marbles at each end. At level IA we obtain very few explanations, but at level IB the active marbles opposite each other are supposd to repel each other through the intermediary of the passive ones as a result of opposite and simultaneous impacts. At level IIA the same idea prevails, but with semi-internal passage. At level IIB there is an anticipation, either of a complete stop, or of a transmission up to the middle marble, which then sends the impulses back each to its own side. Finally, in stage III, the two currents cross each other and, if there are three active marbles on the right and one on the left, then three passive marbles start out on the left and one on the right. We then see that there is a semi-internal transmission starting with level IIA and an internal one in III.

R5 shows a close relationship between the results of R2 and the directions taken by the balls placed either in a single row or with some placed sideways in different positions. In stage I the subject foresees a scattering in all directions, including directions backward or perpendicular to the row. In stage II, oblique directions are foreseen, and the perpendicular ones are quickly eliminated. In stage III the predictions are correct.

R6 opposes a movement by transmission to an inertial movement of two marbles placed on the two sides of an angle-iron set in rotation when hit. We shall return, in § 15, to the inertial movement. Transmission is understood beginning with level IIA, but without at first spelling out the role of the vertical edge of the angle-iron, as is the case in stage III.

As to the interlockings [*engrenages*] of P. Gréco (R7), an action through contact, an immediate transmission, is accepted at stage I, but we must wait for level IIA for an understanding of a continuous interlocking, for level IIB to anticipate and understand the reversals of directions, and for level III for the questions of blocking and unblocking. Wheels connected by a string (R8) give similar results. There is no comprehension of the role of the string at stage I. There is transmission by the string at level IIA, without understanding that the paths traveled by two reference marks on the string or on a same wheel are equal. These paths acquire this

equivalence, "necessarily so," at level IIB, but the string is not yet
the source of a force, which it becomes only in stage III. In connection with the paths taken, let us again quote R9, in which the string
does not turn the wheels but carries two beads, to which it is attached, along a path in the shape of a square. In this situation, in its
simplest form, there is nevertheless no transmission by the string at
level IA, but a remote action of one bead on the other. At level
IB the string is necessary, but if we suggest cutting it at one point
or another, the subject foresees the consequences only very poorly.
At level IIA the mediate transmission is taken for granted, and the
subject even predicts the directions for a model with a string
crossed on a diagonal ($\bowtie$) but, as in R8, he arrives only with
difficulty at the equality of the paths taken by the two beads, even
though they are displaced simultaneously. At level IIB this equivalence becomes necessary, but although the subject foresees quite
naturally the effects of sections of the string on the transmission,
there is still a wavering as to the effect of the string on the segment
between the section and the nearest bead. This last difficult is removed in stage III.

The synchronism between the beginnings of the strictly mediate
transmission and those of the operational transitivity, age 7 to 8,
is found again in other areas but with some small variations, that is,
with the possibility of some slight lags according to the nature of
what is transmitted. For the sound or the vibrations between two
tuning forks placed on a table (R10), the transmissions of stage I
are immediate and at a distance, while in IIA there is a beginning of
mediate transmission, but still external. The sound travels on the
table or through an imaginary wire, not through wood. At level
IIB this is a "current" going through wood or air, and at stage III
a vibration of the air itself, in other respects immobile and no
longer carrying the sound by a transference. R11 deals with mag-
nets and their poles and, in particular, with a suspension of five ball-
bearings held together in a vertical line by a magnet. A clear-cut
opposition appears between stage I, in which the force of the
magnet depends on a "glue" that has all the power, including that
of "blowing" to produce repulsions, and stage II, beginning with age
7, in which the power of the magnet "goes through" the balls that
are suspended from it. It is to be noted that in stage III the action
of the poles is explained by the inequalities of the forces. Two
equal forces, strong or weak, repel each other, therefore increase the
distances, as $(+) \times (+) = (-) \times (-) = (+)$, and two un-

equal forces complete each other, therefore attract each other and shorten the distances, as $(+) \times (-) = (-) \times (+) = (-)$, which resembles the law of signs. On the other hand, when it is a matter of the transmission of a U-shaped tube in water, concerning which we ask what happens to the last drop poured into it (R12), the subjects of level IIA think, like those in IB, that this drop will go through all the liquid, while the push on each successive layer of water is not understood until level IIB.

In connection with the relationships between mediate transmission and transitivity, let us note again two kinds of facts. First of all, in the case of nontransmissions, as in the blockings in Vergnaud's box (R13), where it is a question of taking out one or two rods in succession, so that they no longer prevent the subject from taking out the ones he wants, we find again a clear-cut synchronism between the appearance of these negative transmissions (retentions) in their order of succession and the operational transitivity of the beginnings of stage II. R14 deals with the relationships between operational transitivity and a transfer of matter rather than of movement. Two glasses, *A* and *C,* each three-quarters full and of very different shapes are shown to the child, as well as an empty glass *B* to serve as a middle term, but which we do not mention. After the child has studied the situation, we hide everything behind a screen. When we remove the screen we ask the child what has happened, the red liquid originally in *A* now being in *C* and the green liquid originally in *C* now being in *A.* At the IA level the subject believes that there has been a direct interchange, and is ready to pour, simultaneously or successively, *A* into *C* and *C* into *A,* without using *B.* At the IB level the same thing happens but, as he is about to try it, the subject sees the impossibility of it. The necessary role of glass *B* is understood from the beginning of stage II.

The close connection between operational transitivity and mediate transmission, especially in its semi-internal forms, revealed by these multiple facts, seems therefore evident, except for three differences. The first one is that in an inference such as $A = B$, $B = C$, therefore $A = C$, we go step by step from successive relationships to the remote relationship $(A = C)$, while ordinarily, in transmission, the subject observes a result at the end of a series and reconstructs what happened step by step beginning at the other end. This, however, takes nothing away from the unity of the operational composition. In the second place, and this is what is important, the operational transitivity transmits a simple form, an equivalence or a directed difference, while the mediate causal transmission concerns the passage of a movement, force, etc., that is, of a content in relation to the object. This second difference brings about a third: In the case of logical transitivity, the initial relationships such as $A = B$ and $B = C$ are kept when the subject draws from it the final relationship $A = C$, while in material transmission the movement, etc., that has gone from A to C is gained by C and lost by A, since it deals with the transfer of an element being preserved in the course of a temporal succession but not of a nontemporal form. Are we then to think that it is the logical or formal transmission that genetically brings about the discovery of material transmission or the reverse, or that there is interaction?

Operational transitivity, or transmission of a formal nature,[1] is certainly not created *ex nihilo.* Long before it is recognized and becomes a generalization, the subject can discover in it certain aspects, if only perceptively, when the three elements $A = B = C$ are seen simultaneously before being compared in pairs AB and BC without AC. Moreover, it becomes a generalization only progressively, since the transitivity of weights of equal volume appears only at about age 9 to 10. What is new for the 7- to 8-year-old, in the first transitive compositions that force themselves on his consciousness, is the feeling of logical necessity that characterizes them and that could derive only from a general factor. The closure of the system, for example of seriation, which is up to that time incomplete, but which, once completed by its recurrent method of construction, comprises laws of composition inherent in the system as such, acquires from this fact a character of internal necessity. We can then distinguish in the makeup of operational transitivity two different processes: the definitive structuration according to the laws of the system, and a certain function of coherence or of interlocking [*enchaînement*] consisting of a required unity or of internal equilibrium. This function would be in its origin only a particular case of the need for equilibration,

[1] In the sense of forms as opposed to contents (real or causal transmissions), without alluding to the stage of "formal operations."

but, when there is a sequence of relationships $A = B = C$ . . .
or $A < B < C$ . . . it consists in trying to take into account the
whole interlocking sequence as opposed to particular segments.

However, if the form of a structure cannot be determined by its
content, even though the content and the form remain partly inseparable at the level of concrete operations—and particularly if
necessity is dependent only on form—this function of coherence,
of interlocking, or of unity can only be favored or inhibited, depending on the contents. Let us recall that the general function
of operations is to act on the real by enriching it with settings and
structures permitting its assimilation, and that this general effort
of comprehension, in which the subject must ceaselessly invent and
construct in order to be able to assimilate, is expressed by attempts to transform and not to copy. In such a case, obviously,
the segments of the real most likely to favor the functioning of
operations and to furnish contents for the functional requirements
of interlocking or of coherence will not be those that remain immobile or static, but certainly those in which the real itself is
active and is transformed—in other words, wherever causality is
involved. Putting it another way, the child may on occasion be
interested in seriating for the sake of seriating, in classifying for
the sake of classifying, but, in general, it is when events or phenomena must be explained and goals attained through an organization of causes that operations will be used most.

The solution seems, then, to be the following. The element
common to operational transitivity and causal transmission, while
both are still in the process of being understood, is a function of
totalization or of interlocking that tends to go beyond the starting
point in order to take into account the system as a whole.[2] Such
a functioning would be favored by causal situations, in which the
connection between successive sequences must especially be taken

[2] Note that we find equivalents of such a function at all levels. For example, an animal placed in an unfamiliar environment tends to explore it
as thoroughly as possible. A similar function can also be seen in an experiment on conditioning carried out by A. Rey, in which a guinea pig had the
use of three connected cells, *A*, *B*, and *C*, and a signal announced an
electric shock in *A*. The animal began to jump from *A* to *B* and return to *A*
after the danger was over, and subsequently, without new conditioning or
training, he made the whole trip *ABC*, then *CBA*.

into account, since they are temporal, and where it would serve as a general progressive functioning in the closure of the operational systems, whence the formation of this form of composition, which is transitivity, felt to be necessary at that time. Conversely, and in response to this functional role of contents on the construction of a form, at the concrete level being only the structuring of successive contents, transitivity would rebound on causality by leading to mediate transmission passing through mediators, even if they conserve a certain movement: "semi-internal" form.

In short, the exchange between causality and operation, in this case, would consist of an action of the (causal) contents on a cognitive functioning, which would favor the construction of an operational form reacting in turn on the contents. In other words, the reflexive abstraction that has permitted the construction of transitivity, in which the subject attributes to the object mediate causal transmissions, would have been more easily arrived at through knowledge of a few causal facts such as immediate successive transmissions, the knowledge of these facts having been acquired by physical abstractions, yet reinforcing the need for the closure of the operational structure in the process of formation. Such a process may seem very complicated, but the history of science abounds in cases of this kind. If we dare compare minor ideas with major ones (*si parva licet* . . .), let us recall the circumstances of the invention of infinitesimal calculus. Mathematically, it was virtually on the way to being developed as soon as Descartes' synthesis of algebra (finite) and of geometry (finite) into analytic geometry was effected. All that remained was to extend it into an algebra of the infinite and into a theory of limits. But to take this double step, which could have come from direct generalizations through purely reflexive abstractions, Newton and Leibniz needed the incentive of physical problems, in other words, the suggestion implicit in the contents borrowed from dynamics. Calculus of the infinite, which grew out of this process, does not thereby constitute a product of experience or of simple abstractions drawn from the object alone. Simple abstractions, however, accelerated the process by virtue of their generalizing function, even though this function then returned to the mathematics on which the construction in question was based.[3] Let us also recall the theory of functions involving partial derivatives, the development of which has often been favored by physical analyses, such as those of Euler and D'Alembert in connection with the vibratory cords, of Laplace in starting with the potential, and of Fourier on the subject of heat. A spectacular recent example was Dirac's delta, the initial physical formulation of which was lacking in mathematical rigor but gave birth to one of the most beautiful concepts of contemporary mathematics: the theory of L. Schwartz's distributions.[4]

In general, it cannot be denied that the problems of physical causality have frequently given rise to mathematical inventions by, not a copy of the real, but a kind of operational reconstruction of a phenomenon the knowledge of which was previously dictated by experience. There is therefore nothing surprising in finding on a smaller scale such processes from the very beginning of the acquisition of operational and physical knowledge in the child.

5. Immediate Transmissions and Immediate Inferences. Meaning of Attributions

If causality played a role in the formulation of transitivity by facilitating interlocking in the preoperational stages, it may be helpful to add a few remarks on the relationships between the most elementary causal and logical structures at levels where they remain relatively undifferentiated and where the inferences as well as the transmissions remain immediate.

[3] J. B. Grize has, however, shown that even in the field of mathematics, derivatives have for a long time retained a temporal significance and that it was not until the beginning of the nineteenth century that time was definitely eliminated from differential calculus.

[4] Whence the dedication that Lighthill wrote in his work, *Fourier Analysis and Generalized Functions:* "To Dirac, who saw that it must be true; Laurent Schwartz, who proved it; and George Temple, who showed how simple it could be made."

We observe such immediate inferences starting with the sensori-motor level in the interpretation of familiar indices. A baby at the breast who shows impatience at feeding time calms down as soon as he sees his mother appear, which in verbal terms would be translated as "Mother, therefore nursing." Again, when he sees a hanging object, he will stretch out his hand, not to take it but to make it swing, which is the equivalent of the inference "hanging, therefore swinging." It is immediately evident that in such behavior there intervenes both a form that the subject is intelligent enough to see, which is the inferential or implicating link in the sense of simple, significant, or broad implications as opposed to propositional implications, and a content that is causal, since the combination of "Mother" or "hanging object" with the action itself produces causally the nursing or the swinging. If the causal connection discovered and performed in the action itself is not sufficient to assure the development of the ability to make inferences, because the latter depends on the cognitive activity of the subject and on the system of the *schèmes* of recognition and generalization, then it is clear that this internal functioning of the intelligent assimilation is no less favored and is constantly reinforced by the causal situations in which the anticipations are followed by effective controls (the success or failure of the swinging depending on whether the hanging object was really a mobile or not, etc.).

This does not mean that all the immediate inferences of the preoperational levels have a causal content. They can serve as classifiers. For example, pipe implies Father, even though in the majority of cases what interests the subject in the objects is what he can produce, by himself or as an instrument of the action itself, therefore their causal aspects. But in the realm of the causal, it goes without saying that the functioning of intelligence, in its efforts to anticipate or comprehend, is all the more stimulated and developed when the problems posed by the real are more varied and more interesting. As a result, we have a permanent functional stimulation that reinforces the development of *schèmes* in their totality, that is, in all categories (classes, relationships, etc.), but naturally especially in those that may be structurally analogous to the relationships involved in the causal problem under consideration.

In this respect, when, in the problems of transmission the subject reduces the mediate transmissions to a succession of linked immediate transmissions, obviously the IB level abounds in the possibilities of exercising what we called in § 4 a function of totalization or interlocking that can lead to the construction of transitivity.

We must make another observation in order to avoid possible ambiguities. It is clear that, if causality favors the functional exercise of intelligence, the operational constructions of that intelligence still proceed by "reflexive" and not by physical or simple abstractions. From this, it follows that the final operational structure, once used in the causal explanation, is clearly attributed to objects and is not drawn directly from them. However, and this must be emphasized, nothing prevents the construction of the operational structure, for example transitivity, from taking place simultaneously with the solution of the causal problem. The structure in question is in effect a form, and, as such, is constructed by the activity of the subject in order to structure a given content. Whether this content is at first relative to classes such as transitivity of nestings, or to relationships such as transitivity of equivalences or of graded differences, and that it is then only causal, such as transitivity of transmissions, or whether the construction has its inception when the subject is presented with a causal content that can be generalized when he encounters others, is not important and can vary according to the subject. In each of these cases the form is due to a reflexive abstraction and the content is known by simple abstraction, in such a way that the operational form is either only applied or else attributed to objects (contents). If the construction of the form began as a result of a causal problem, this attribution is then instantaneous, that is, it takes place at the same time as the construction itself, just as in other cases it is only the application that is simultaneous with the construction of forms.

As for the difference between application and attribution, the criterion is simple. When the subject is engaged in classifications, seriations, enumerations or measures, etc., it is he who acts, whereas the objects allow themselves to be acted upon without imposing on the subject any one operation more than another.

When, on the other hand, an operational composition is attributed to the object, such as transitivity in the case of transmission, it is the objects that act; that is, they themselves guarantee the transmission, and it is up to the subject to accept the facts. Of course, the subject retains his own activity; that is, an attributed operation is always simultaneously applied and attributed to the object, but the converse is not true because an operation can be applied to objects without being attributed to them. For example, ten pebbles are ten only if a subject counts them in correspondence with other sets, whereas a movement is transmitted without the intervention of the subject. The child (and not only he), believes that the number is in the pebbles, just as he believes that a mountain has always had its name. When he attributes transitivity to the movement of marbles, he puts himself in their place without suspecting that, in fact, he is imagining, just like the physicist, that they operate like him. But in the first case, the error of attribution detracts nothing from the validity of the enumeration, which depends only on correspondences independently of their ideological interpretation, whereas the attribution of an operation to a causal process is subject to experimental control and to continuous progress in the refinement of the model, and therefore of the interpretation.

In this respect we should note particularly that, in the case of the attribution of operational transitivity to the mediate transmission of the movement, the first includes a necessary invariant due to its reversibility, whereas the second does not automatically entail a quantitative conservation of the movement, nor *a fortiori* of the energy, and will reach that point only in stage III.

There is another observation to be made. The attribution of operations to a physical system then considered as causal may not necessarily be favored by the convergence of the external objective data and the operational tendencies of the subject. On the contrary, it often happens that the contradictions between the observed facts and the chosen operational models require a modification of the latter. In this case the very effort necessary to the resulting coherence engenders a new system of operations attributable to objects, from the fact alone that the elimination of contradictions implies a play of inferences which, by their very deductive nature, constitutes a new operational structure. It is thus that in the case of the interlocking of immediate transmissions of movements, at the IB level, the chosen model is in contradiction with the fact that the marbles do not start moving one after the other, from which arises a new construction founded on mediateness and transitivity and that leads to the semi-internal transmissions of stage II: The movement "goes through" the marbles at the same time that it displaces them but only slightly. We shall return to this formative role of the contradictions in paragraph VI of the conclusions.

6. *Symmetries, Compensations, and Reversibility*

Another precocious form of composition raises the same problem even more sharply. This is the compensation of quantities, for example of weights, in situations of equilibrium, comparable in the causal realm to the fundamental, operational *schèmes* of reversibility. Three sets of factors intervene in such compositions. First, there is factual data, drawn by simple abstraction from the experiences of the body itself or from daily observations in the manipulation of objects. Second, there is the operational structure of reversibility, drawn by reflexive abstraction from the self-regulations of the subject. Finally, there is a general functional tendency of the subject toward equilibration, source of self-regulations, and therefore, in the final analysis, of the *schème* of the reversible operations but by which it could very well be favored by causal actions. That is one of the questions to be discussed. Indeed, if a simple relationship of causality is irreversible, the states of equilibrium, which are explained causally in the same manner as transformations, are characterized by possible operations, and therefore by actual or mechanical reversibility, namely, equal operations in opposite directions. We therefore see that this field of compensations is one of those in which either the exogenous and endogenous factors or physical causality and operation can be intermeshed in the most intimate and complex way.

Let us first recall the facts. From the age of 4 (R15) the subjects anticipate that a ruler pushed perpendicularly to the edge of a table will fall if it goes beyond the table for a little more than half its length. Before the age of 7, however, weight is not taken into account, and the term "long" or "big" end is used. Here it is more than likely a case of a symmetry inspired by the actions of the body itself, because if we use a thin rectangular board (R16) instead of a ruler, we note that, until stage II, the board pushed forward at a 45° angle and no longer perpendicular to the edge of the table will fall in a line predetermined by its small median, and not by an oblique line corresponding to the edge of the table, taking into account the equivalence between the part supported by the table and the part not supported by it. In the same way, an open knife is placed with the midpoint on the edge of the table without taking into account the difference in weight between the handle and the blade, etc. Then again, although the child anticipates from level IB onward that a balance will be achieved with two similar plugs of equal weights, that is, symmetry, he no longer anticipates it with four plugs, two on each side, or with unlike objects of similar weights.

The problem is shown to be even further from solution when, with a circular support, where the point of equilibrium is marked by a ring in the center to which strings are attached and which will move when the weights are unequal, *n* weights suspended by a string on one side must be balanced by as many weights tied to a string hanging on the other side (R17). We must wait until stage II (about age 7) for the subject to be sure of compensation by equalization of weights, with no consideration of directions. Likewise, the problems of counterweights are not mastered in stage I when an object is held back or lifted. In experiments of practical intelligence in which the child has to hang a metal basket (R18), we see him, until about age 7, use any object on which to hook the basket, even a pencil standing up in a light box, without taking into consideration the particular weights. In the case of a cart on an incline, which can be pulled up or held back according to the counterweights suspended on the other side of the pulley, the subjects of stage I see no stable relationship between the two weights in question [1] (R19). It is true that in stage I the composition of weights is not additive, varying according to whether they are placed

---

[1] These problems of counterweights are physically more complex because the conditions of balance vary with the slope. But of course we limit ourselves here to the simple comprehension of facts that a certain weight is needed to hold back an object, and a greater weight is necessary to lift it.

higher or lower, etc., but the facts that we have just recalled are concerned with equivalent heights, where the compensations for the equalization of quantities are still not understood at stage I. On the other hand, in these various experiments, understanding comes at stage II, at least when the weights are at equal heights (see R16; see also the neutral equilibrium of R20 when two equal weights suspended vertically from unequal heights are supposed to move to reach the same height).

The problem, then, is as follows. Additive compositions and quantifications, as well as the handling of reversibility deemed necessary, appear at the level of concrete operations. From the causal point of view, the disequilibrium resulting from the inequality of the balanced weights, or the compensations needed to reach equilibrium by equalization, stem from the same structure but are attributed to the object and are no longer inherent in the classes, relationships, or numbers constructed by the subject. Does it then follow that the causal model is only the product of a projection in the real of operational *schèmes* that the subject attains at this level of development, or that these *schèmes* grow out of the physical experience or, again, that there intervene interactions analogous to those we saw in § 4?

Let us first try to reduce the given of the problem to its most general form, since in the preceding data we encounter notions as varied as symmetry, compensation, reversibility, and equilibrium. Let us recall that operational reversibility can be expressed in the form of a symmetry. It is even the language currently used to describe group structure. The operation of P^{-1}, the inverse of P, will be, so to speak, its symmetrical correspondent. Second, a physical system is in balance when its probable movements, or operations, compensate each other, which leads us to a symmetry. On the other hand, any compensation whatever, whether it is an active one by the subject trying to cancel the effects of an external disturbance, or a physical one precociously understood—such as increasing the speed of a ball in motion by changing the incline or the height of the starting point to compensate for an increase in the mass of a ball at rest—amounts to equalizing two opposite actions, thereby reestablishing a symmetry. *A fortiori,* the same applies to the equalizations of weights or sizes mentioned above.

It is then evident that the subject discovers or learns to recognize a considerable number of symmetries or compensations long before he reaches the operational reversibility considered necessary, and therefore also long before the valid, causal compositions of stage II corresponding to these reversible operations. Without speaking of perceptible symmetries, starting with the sensori-motor level we can point to multiple behaviors that are compensatory or tending to symmetry, such as removing an obstacle in the way of a goal, straightening out a slipping object or reestablishing the balance of the body itself, placing or throwing an object to one side of the subject after having thrown it on the other side, etc. The symmetries cited above, that is, the anticipation of a ruler falling when more than half of it extends beyond the end of a table, the equilibrium on scales or a swing, etc., are then only particular cases fitting into a long series of experiences.

At first, the result is that the reversible operations do not arise *ex nihilo,* but constitute, as we have often insisted elsewhere, the ultimate limit of self-regulations when the precorrection of errors or the precompensation of disturbances succeeds to postcorrection or postcompensation, as a result of actions already carried out or experienced. Then, obviously, the causal compensations of stage II of an almost operational form are set up by the symmetries and compensations approximated in the preoperational stage I. On the other hand, it is doubtful that these primitive attempts—still full of gaps and somewhat contradictory—are sufficient to explain the progress in stage II in this area of causality, and the influence of operational reversibility with its quantitative compensations seems necessary. But, here again, if this causal composition, starting with stage II, constitutes an operational composition attributed to objects, it is nevertheless true that, throughout the whole of stage I, the compensatory regulations of the subject are very likely reinforced or facilitated by his causal experiences. Indeed, it seems evident that experience and especially the exercise of compensations become much more concrete in areas where failures or simply difficulties result from a resistance of the things themselves than in the areas of reasoning, where the noncompensations become evident simply through errors that may not be recognized as such. This action of the physical experience on self-regulations, sources of reversibility, does not naturally mean that this reversibility is only abstracted from the real but simply that the long, endogenous process ending in reversible operations is constantly reinforced by the reactions to material problems and the necessity of finding a solution to them.

In the final analysis, the common source of operational reversibility and of compensations peculiar to causal actions is naturally found in the organism, since the latter is at the same time the seat of multiple physico-chemical compensations through which it partakes of the laws of matter and of a homeostatic activity more and more differentiated, from which ensue a growing number of readjustments, including those of conduct characterizing the behavior of the subject. But we shall return to this in paragraph X of the conclusions.

7. *The Internal Compositions of Bodies*

A realm particularly rich in combinations of reflexive abstractions, sources of operations, and physical or simple abstractions that come into the solution of every causal problem is that of the notions formed by the child of the compositions of bodies and of the changing states of matter. The development of these explanations presents a double interest for our general problem.

In the first place, a physical phenomenon can, by its very nature, suggest the use of an operational composition in an additive form, resulting in a precocious "attribution," while in other areas that composition will come later because nothing in the objects considered seems to impose it. Thus, when sugar is dissolved, the fact that the initial piece visibly disintegrates into little pieces and these into smaller and smaller particles causes the subjects, from the IIA level on, to assume that water separates them and, from the IIB level on, that they end up by existing in an invisible form when they do not become syrup, and also that, when they come back together again, they add up to the initial whole.[1] On the

[1] See J. Piaget and B. Inhelder, *Le développement des quantités physiques chez l'enfant*, ch. IV.

other hand, such a corpuscular model is generally formed only around age 11 to 12 for bodies that do not dissolve or for anything involving changes in the state of matter, the rapidity and qualitative modifications of which present other problems. This contrast, between the dissolving of sugar, which is understood from age 7 to 8, and the other situations mastered only in stage III, recalls the difference between the semi-internal mediate transmissions of stage II, in which movements are ascribed to objects, and the purely internal transmission of stage III, when the subject admits the existence of nonperceptible realities such as the passage of a current in the case of transmission or the corpuscles in the present case.

Another interesting aspect of additive compositions, ascribed by the subject to some bodies as opposed to others, is the relationship of dependency that exists between the notions and the forms of the activity itself. Thus, the manipulation of objects, which calls for an active control, rapidly entails the idea that solids are com-posed of macroscopic parts stuck together and that liquids are composed of moving parts. However, since seeing demands no such controls, except for the act of focusing, there is no light that goes from the object to the eye or from a lamp to the bright spot projected at a distance, but, on the contrary, the look is a quasi-substantial reality that goes from the eye to meet the objects.

With this in mind, let us recall in broad outline the facts observed. For the experiment on sugar, taken up again in R21 in reference to the actual mechanism of dissolving, and for the dispersion of a coal pellet in water (R22), the evolution is very clear. At the beginning (stage I) there is no conservation of matter, the sugar disappears and, in the case of the coal, the water simply becomes black; nor is there conservation of the granules, which become liquid before they disappear or color the water. The dissolving of the sugar is at first (level IA) attributed to the simple cracking by the spoon or to the fall of the original piece. In stage II, there is conservation of matter and of granules, in the form of little solids, with the exception that they become liquid or "color" the water, the sum of these granules being equivalent to the whole original piece. However, these granules, which would be visible with a magnifying glass, do not themselves contain smaller elements. In stage III they are drawn as if they contained ultragranules as ultimate units. An-

other study designed to relate internal and external compositions
(R23) consisted in having the child pour a liquid and a certain
amount of fine gravel onto a dinner plate and asking him why
there is a difference between the two, and in having him dip sticks
in water, oil, molasses, cubed sugar, powder, or flour, in order to
have him explain the actions of wetting and sticking. In stage I the
water runs out because it is "fine" or "thin" and because it "slides,"
etc., whereas the pebbles stay in place because they are "thick" or
because "they can't be broken up, the milk is already broken up,"
and they are unbreakable because the pieces are tight in the sense
of being well stuck together. As for the actions of wetting and sticking, they are explained only tautologically. Water wets "because it's
not made hard, otherwise it wouldn't be water," and bodies that
stick do so because "it's a little sticky." In stage II, however, we
note a triple progress:

1. The flow of water and the piling up of pebbles depend on the
causal actions between the parts of the whole. In the case of pebbles, the lower layers support the upper, whereas the layers of water
mingle: "It goes on top and under," "it cannot stay up," etc.

2. The difference in resistance depends on the fact that "liquids
move all by themselves," whereas pebbles are made of sand, crumbs,
or powder but are held together as a whole, like a "sort of cement,"
etc.

3. The actions of sticking or wetting are then explained by analogous models. Fine things wet without sticking; "thick things hold
together best," like molasses, the drops of which are "thicker."
As for powdered sugar, it adheres to the stick because it "hooks,"
while in sugar cubes "the granules have little points and they stick
together with the little points," etc.

Finally, in stage III, these semimacroscopic and semimicroscopic
models yield to strictly corpuscular structures, but with difficulty in
making homogeneous the ultimate elements of liquids and solids,
particularly because of the continuous character of the first, so that
we get formulas such as (12;5): drops "are like nested inside each
other," while grains in the pebbles "stay together," that is, are
bunched together.

There is little doubt that the evolution we have just retraced
depends closely on that of additive operations. In stage I, when
on the operational level there is no conservation of the wholes
according to the way in which the elements are brought together,

and therefore no reversible operation of addition, neither is there a corpuscular model, except in the form of macroscopic pieces, nor conservation of pieces or granules once they are visible. Sugar at first dissolves because it is cracked (R21) before it is destroyed. Coal disperses in the form of simple color, etc. On the other hand, in stage II, where the assemblings, or additions, and the conservation of the whole are formed operationally, we see developing, parallel to each other, semimicroscopic corpuscular models in such a way that the totality of the granules is equivalent to the whole piece, and the elements hold together, more or less, in diverse ways. In stage III this additive composition is generalized to the microscopic point of being unobservable. Moreover, it is not simply a question of operations by the subject applied to objects, but, in fact, of attributed operations, since it is the elements of the objects themselves that are understood as dissociating themselves or coming together in a casual way.

However, as far as the relationships between the operations and this causality are concerned, the problem is a little different from what we have seen for transitivity or reversibility. Without doubt, like these preceding operational forms, the additive compositions are prepared by preoperational behavior, consisting of the material and the manual actions of assembling. Only it is difficult to see what, in the experience of the child, could constitute spontaneous assemblings stemming from the objects themselves, independent of human actions. The stones of a wall are fitted together by the mason; those of a rocky cliff seem always to have been there, except in cases so commonly thought to be artificial in stage I. We therefore see scarcely any action of causality between objects in additive operations.

It is true that, if we put in opposition to additions or logico-arithmetic assemblings, which bear on separate objects, the infra-logical or partitive additions that concern the continuous as opposed to separate objects, the situation changes somewhat. The initial operation is, then, in effect, dividing or sectioning, while the assembling of parts or pieces in a total object is its inverse operation. It seems that in the physical and causal experience of objects that the child can have at his level, independently of his own actions, the sectioning is more frequent than the assembling,

which could facilitate the preoperational functioning of the divisions. However, sectioning is one thing, and the assembling of the
separated parts with conservation of the whole is something else
again. At the IB level of the notions on the dissolving of sugar,
the subject no longer says, as he did in IA, that the piece of sugar
broke in falling, etc. He begins to admit that the water has contributed to pulling apart the preexistent granules, but even then he
does not arrive at the concept of an addition that conserves the
whole. The very reversibility of the division seems, therefore, to
make it more difficult to find causal incitements in the real that
would favor the development of corresponding operations. In
the last analysis, the latter seem to play a rather fundamental role,
as is demonstrated in the history of science, by the influence of
additive and even numerical (Pythagoras) compositions in the
formation of Greek atomism.

On the other hand, if the causality peculiar to the objects themselves seems scarcely suitable for accelerating the development of
additive operations, it goes without saying that the preoperational
actions consisting of assembling or separating solids are at once
of a dynamic, kinetic, spatial, and logico-arithmetic nature, since
these solids are subjected to material displacements that move
them closer together or farther apart, etc. In this sense it is clear
that causality favors the formation of additive compositions to the
point where we can wonder if a person who lives in a state of
absolute immobility, assuming it were possible, would arrive at
a concept of additions and subtractions. But in this case it is a
question of a causality peculiar to the action of the subject as well
as to his interactions with objects, and not a causality limited to
the connections between the objects themselves.

The same thing must be said of the case in which the geometric experience comes closest to that of addition. The group
of displacements in fact dictates the additive composition of the
latter, since the sum of any two of them is still a displacement:
$a + a' = b$. This is so true that the advocates of a primitive and
extralogical intuition of the number or of the iteration $+n$ or
$n + 1$, like Poincaré, sometimes saw in the succession of walking
steps a sort of material prototype of this iteration. However, geometric operations are operations of the subject as well as modifica-

tions of the object. When the subject himself performs displacements of the objects he handles as well as of his own movements
—when he physically starts these operations—then it is certainly
a question of causal as well as of operational actions, but of a
causality inherent in the action itself, and therefore of a case
particular to the one just considered.

8. *Changes in States of Matter*

If macroscopic additive compositions are attributed only with
difficulty to nonobservable corpuscular models, the same will apply
a fortiori to the changes in states of matter, although to the additive operations are added only spatial operations of displacement
and condensation. The reexamination of our hypotheses on this
subject will thus be all the more interesting, but first let us review
the facts.

R24 deals with the fusion of cetaceum. In the course of stage I
the subject at first refuses to consider the liquid as the same substance as the initial powder: "water shows up when it is heating"
or "it made water," but without any consideration of the transformation of a permanent matter. In the course of stage II (age 7 to
10), this identity is recognized, but with no granules remaining in
the liquid because "they are changed into water," etc. There are
no quantitative conservations between the two states but, when
the liquid returns to the initial state, we find the same quantities. Nic
(8;8) says that it will be the same weight "because there are as
many granules" as before the fusion, and Pan (9) specifies that "if
there were a million before, now there is also a million and it is the
same weight," and that, in spite of the fact that between the two
states "they melted." In stage III we witness the beginning of a
permanence of invisible granules in the liquid, but less than in the
case of sugar, which dissolves in water; this time the solid is often
changed into liquid. On the other hand, if we bring to the subject's
attention the conservation of weight from one state to the other,
the corpuscular model is markedly reinforced by it. Rus (10;11)
says, for example, "out of all these little granules there will be a
liquid coming out and there'll be no more little granules." We weigh

it. Same weight! "There are no fewer little granules. There is the same amount . . . because we didn't take any away!" Bes (11;6), after having said that the granules "melted," changes her mind as a result of our asking the question of conservation of weight: "Oh yes, there will always be the same number . . . you heat it and there is the same number. You cool it and there is still the same number." The transformations of the paraffin of a candle (R25) give rise to the same reactions among the youngest subjects. In stage I the melted "wax" is no longer a part of the candle but "its juice," etc. On the other hand, at level IIA they are the same pieces, "bumps," "barks," etc., but "stuck" or "mixed" in the solid and separated, then melted, in the liquid. At level IIB the idea of "tight" is added to this macroscopic corpuscular model, but the elements still end up by melting. In stage III the two final steps are that the corpuscles stay invisible in the liquid, and especially that they "move—it's like the marbles that we spill on the ground," while in the solid state "they are very close together" and can "no longer move."

As for the passage of the liquid to the gaseous state, we first analyzed it with a Franklin distillation apparatus and with sulfuric ether (R26), where the passage of steam is invisible even though it is taking place along a transparent tube. In this case, even though the subjects of level IB see the liquid decreasing in one of the flasks, appearing and then increasing in the other, they refuse to admit to a passage of matter and prefer to believe that the water each time comes from the outside, even though the apparatus is obviously closed. At level IB there is a passage of matter, but it is still not understood. At level IIA the same holds true, with the addition of conservation of matter but without any idea of evaporation. Evaporation arises at age 9 to 10 (IIB), but with some hesitation between the ideas of transformation and emanation. Finally, in stage III steam is conceived as "tiny pieces of water" that "are brought together more tightly" in the liquid state.

Moreover, let us recall that in a study (R27) bearing on steam and odor, the subjects of stage I believe that the steam comes out of the water but without quite having the same identity, and that odor remains attached to the scented body, wihout moving up to the nose. In level IIA odor is a part of the air or of the steam which moves, and the latter is already made up of "thin layers of water," etc. At level IIB the odor results from mixing with the air, which circulates, and "something inside" coming out of the bodies, but without yet constituting corpuscles as such. Finally, in stage III the odor as well as the steam is formed from ultimate elements, "granules," "points," etc., which in certain cases escape the dichotomy solid–liquid, therefore, granules or drops, but present the characteristic of "going in all directions" instead of remaining tightly together.

We see that, despite the precociousness of the concepts of ice, which familiar experience shows to be "water stuck together" or "tight," etc., and despite daily experiences that dictate these ideas of tight and spaced (but, naturally, on the macroscopic level as opposed to the corpuscular, "tightness" characterizing in stage III the idea of density), the changes in the state of matter create, for the subject, problems that remain insoluble for a long time. At the outset, we even note the refusal to admit an identity of substance between the alternate states, and the tendency, at first insuperable, to substitute the idea of emanation for that of transformation. However, the operations involved in the final explanations are only very elementary, except for the difficulty, considerable though it is, of attributing them to imperceptible micro-objects. They are reduced, on the one hand, to simple additive compositions, and, on the other, to the notion that in going from a solid to a liquid to a gas, the particles get farther apart and become more mobile. Now, when we come to macroscopic elements, not only are these three operations common from the beginning of level IIA, but they also correspond to multiple material preoperational actions, the simultaneously causal and quasioperational meaning of which we saw at the end of § 7. The fact that the same operations are so difficult to attribute to objects when they are on such a small scale that they cannot be observed, when action on individual corpuscles becomes impossible, seems to confirm retroactively that, in cases where everything can be seen, the action plays a causal role and is at the same time a source of operations in the development of this type of causality through additive compositions.

With this in mind, let us point out again that this form of explanation amounts not only to attributing to objects assemblings or dissociations of a general or indeterminate character, but also that the attribution goes as far as encompassing the numerical ratios themselves. The whole number results from a synthesis of order and inclusion appearing at the end of natural numbers or when the subject establishes a correspondence between one element in one set and another element in the second set or vice versa. As such, the number intervenes in an essential way in most of the operations applied to the object. But, when in stage II the subjects Nic and Pan admit that the number of granules of cetaceum will be found again as soon as they return to the solid state, even though they disappeared during fusion, or when Rus, in stage III, seeing the weight of the liquid conserved in that of the solid, concludes that the number of granules is constant in the liquid itself, these numbers no longer stem from applied operations, but from a so-called attribution. The meaning of this is evident: Between the granules of state A and those of state B, or even of a return to A' with a momentary disappearance in B, there exists a correspondence of one element in one set to another element in the second set that is no longer brought about by the subject, but that belongs to objects as such and is presented in the form of either a continuous identity or a resurgence of identity after a phase of disappearance. This numerical correspondence, therefore, is in such a case attributed to the action of the objects themselves.

9. The Problems of Direction with Thrusts or Pulls

In the transitivities, compensations, and additive compositions examined thus far, the problem was one of relationships between causality and general forms of operational coordination. We have noted that, if the causal explanation in such cases always results in an attribution of operations to the object, the development of the latter comprises no less a number of facilitations coming from the physical experience through the intermediary of a functioning more or less reinforced or inhibited depending on the contents to be structured. When we come to directions, we find new problems, since we are no longer concerned with so many general coordinations and relationships between the operational forms and the experimental contents, but rather are concerned with spatial operations, the peculiar characteristic of which is the construction of forms of which some correspond, in other respects, to similar forms existing in the objects themselves and subject to being reached perceptively or through physical experience.

We now face three principal problems. The first is inherent in geometric operations: the problem of relationships between reflexive abstraction, the source of these operations, and simple or physical abstraction, from which comes, in part, the knowledge of material space or of objects. The second problem is met often in areas where causal explanation interferes with a particular spatial structuration: Does the latter direct the former or vice versa, or are there interactions and, if so, in what forms? The third problem takes us back to our general concern: in cases in which causality is linked to spatial coordination, must we again say that it results from an attribution of operations to the object, or does its constitution depend only on the data of experience?

Some results make it possible to define more accurately the last two of these problems. By having the subject push rod B oblique or perpendicular to active rod A, which touches one of their extremities (R28), we note that the subjects of stage I predict with difficulty only displacements without rotation for the passive rod. At level IIA the partial rotation of B in relation to A is understood, but without coordinating the displacement with the external system of reference. At the IIB level the coordination is attempted, but with little success. At stage III the two systems of reference are coordinated, and the result of the thrust correctly predicted. An analogous experiment using thin rectangular boards pushed at different points by a needle or a pencil (R29) gave the same results at level IA, displacements without rotations, but the rotations, without coordinations with the displacements, are anticipated from the beginning of level IB, doubtless because, in utilizing two rods similar to R28, we let the subject put more emphasis on the direction of the active rod. At level IIA the coordination is attempted with varying success. At level IIB it is successful through trial and error, and at stage III it is successful at the first attempt. If we conduct the same experiment utilizing pull (R30), we find analogous results, but with more precocious references to the role of the weight of the different parts of the object pulled. Again, in level IIA the action of pulling adds weight to the part touched, as it did in the case of thrust; but from the IIB level it is the biggest segment, in relation to the point of impact, which is the heaviest. Likewise, if instead of a rectangle we provide a triangular board, then in order to push or pull the object toward him, the subject no longer chooses the point of impact in the middle of the base, but on a line dividing it in equal weights. On the other hand, a rectangular board provided with an off-center hole is still pushed in the middle, and it is only in stage III that the direction is predicted in terms of weights—and these weights are judged in terms of volume.

These first facts already show that the direction of the objects pushed or pulled can be predicted or interpreted in two ways according to whether the accent is placed on geometric movements or whether the active forces are combined with the resistance (weights) of the passive mobile. The first of these two processes either leads to errors or else seems sufficient, but only from the point of view of prediction and not of explanation. With a second group of data, in which a push is applied to the base of four dowel sticks either parallel or in the shape of a cross (R31), or to sets of three dowels with n articulated rods (R32), we find ourselves faced with a new factor: the intervention of a single operation with collective movements (R31) or the transmission of the movement from one element to the next. In the case of the sticks, they are at first (stage I) interpreted spatially as a single whole, for example, ||||, in such a way that a moving action pushing them from right to left at their base will bend them toward the left in the direction of the movement itself, even if the subject (level IB) is capable of predicting the correct direction for a single element. In stage II this correct direction is predicted for the four sticks. In stage IIA, however, there are still some who consider the figure as a whole, and therefore the problem of the sticks being perpendicular to the sides of a square tablet, which causes them to turn, is not yet solved for lack of an understanding of the detail of the action of the four angles. We do not get answers to all the questions until stage III. With the articulated rods of R32, where a push against the lower vertical rod makes the horizontal rod turn around a screw in the middle and pushes the upper vertical rod pulled by the preceding one, the apparatus ⌐ prompts correct predictions and explanations as early as level IIA. On the other hand, if we add elements with various combinations of pushes and pulls, we observe two methods. One, which is successful, consists of following the articulations step by step, which makes the anticipation dependent on the comprehension of dynamics. The other, which fails or delays solutions, consists of studying the whole figure, looking for symmetries, contrasts, or analogies that depend more on configurations than on dynamics.

R33, 34, and 35 deal with the impact of one ball on the side of another, or of one marble on the side of a round box, the two problems being that of the direction in which the passive mobile *B* starts out in relation to the point of impact and that of the active mobile *A* after the impact. In stage I the direction of *B* allows *A* to go farther, and the latter continues on its way or "goes elsewhere." At level IIA, ball *B* goes in the direction opposite that of the impact, but without taking into account the detailed variations of the point of impact. The direction of *A* after the impact remains, in general, poorly anticipated. After the gradual progress of level IIB, but still without realizing that the path taken by *B* goes through its center ["it is only the point where it touches which is important," says a subject (11;0)], stage III is characterized by two points understood: that of the role of the center of *B,* and a correct deviation of *A* due to the reaction of *B,* which "drives it away," "sends it back," etc., in a way symmetrical to the impact received. Briefly, the directions seem clearly subordinated to the development of the explanation of dynamics rather than dictated by geometric reasons.

On the other hand, in the case of a fixed wall, we may wonder if the progressive discovery of the equality of angles of incidence and of reflection is not a matter of pure spatial symmetry. Therefore, we have taken up again, from the point of view of causality, the induction of this law with the former experiments of B. Inhelder when a ball hits a wall (R36) and with reflections in a mirror (R37). As far as the wall is concerned, it is at first (stage I) only an obstacle to be avoided by the ball: whence the anticipation of curved trajectories not touching it so the ball will not stop. In level IIA the wall changes the direction of the ball by sending it to the opposite side, but without consideration of angles because the variations of reflection depend on the force with which it is thrown or on the "resumption of impetus" after the impact. In level IIB, on the other hand, the wall is no longer a mediator, and the subject looks for the covariations between the directions of incidence and of reflection. Finally, in stage III, equality is postulated and often explained by the relationships between the action and the reaction. As far as the reciprocities of the images in the mirror are concerned, dynamics is no longer involved when people are in different positions (R37). However, the understanding of directions is still linked to causal interpretations, whether the "reflection" "collides" with the mirror (Bor at 8;6) or whether "your reflection gets here ($\nearrow$) and my look gets there ($\nwarrow$)."

Let us also review two studies from the point of view of the relationships between causality and systems of natural coordinates, one on movements and motor controls necessary to maintain in a vertical position a long stick on a fingertip (R38), and the second (R39) on the reasons for water levels being horizontal. The first of these analyses shows that, although we find successful results in practice at any age, at first the explanations are centered only on the action itself. In stage III, however, they are on the object, about which Sop (10;8) says that "the bottom must stay under the point," and that is so "because there is a lot of weight on top," according to Sed (12;1); thus the balance requires the vertical position. The subjects do not anticipate the horizontality of water, but once they have noticed it, they explain it by the action of the container on the liquid, which corresponds to the relationships between the water and its container by means of which they anticipate the orientation of the level (oblique, etc.) without any connection to external references. On the contrary, the subjects who could anticipate the horizontality, and therefore who have recourse geometrically to these external references, explain it by the downward flow or by the weight of the water, which excludes a sloping level for reasons of balance, but which presumes the independence of the liquid in relation to the container and thus corresponds causally to relationships inside or outside the container.

Finally, let us mention a study (R40) on the direction taken by drops or trickles of water in terms of the longitudinal movement of a tube with three holes. We question the child on the directions of the fall of a single drop, then on the continuous trickle of water and on what happens when one starts and then abruptly stops the tube. At level IA there is no difference in the directions according to whether the tube is immobile or in motion. At level IB the water goes in the same direction as the tube, but by a lack of differentiation and not by transmission, while at level IIA it goes backwards. After intermediary reactions in level IIB, the responses of level IIIA take into consideration the two systems of reference and give the

proper trajectory for a drop of water: forward, then vertical. But it
is not until level IIIB that the trajectory of the trickle of water is
understood as being "dragged along."

From these data we can at first conclude that in all the cases
studied, the geometric structuring of directions is linked to dynamics, but with perhaps two reservations as to the nature of this
connection. In the first place, we could suppose that the spatial
factor alone intervenes in the cases of simple anticipations without
causal explanation, for example, in the case where the thin rectangular board pushed perpendicularly to the left of the median
point of its base is supposed to move "in a straight line," without
rotation and subject to the direction given by the moving agent, or
even when the forecast is correct and the subject anticipates, without knowing why, a rotation of a few degrees because the point of
propulsion is "not in the middle." But if this is the way things
happen, we should first talk about spatial operations, or preoperational functions, only "applied" and not "attributed" to the
object, because of the lack of causality. However, it is probable
that this would involve only borderline cases, because the lack of
explicit explanation by the subject does not mean that there is no
implicit causality. The fact that a push intervenes, the push of a
material, solid object whose shape cannot change, can lead the
subject to attributing to the push various powers, among which
are those of keeping the object "straight" or making it turn.

In the second place, to suppose that there is always a connection between spatial structuring and dynamic explanation does not
mean that the latter is always valid. There are therefore two cases
to be recognized—whether the explanation is valid or whether it is
not—and even three cases, because, if it is not valid, the anticipation itself can be right or wrong. In the case of a correct forecast
and a wrong explanation, when, for example, the child does foresee the rotation of the rectangular thin piece of wood but thinks
that the part pushed or pulled becomes heavier from that very fact,
even though it is smaller, we could consider it a gain of the geometric over the dynamic. Only in the case of wrong anticipations
and explanations, as in the case of the thin piece of wood of the
same form but with a large hole on one side which the subject

pushes in its middle to make it "go straight," is this primacy of the spatial due to a deficiency of the explanation of dynamics; that is, the "size" and especially the perimeter of the rectangle are judged more important than the distribution of the weights. As a matter of fact, sometimes the spatial guides the dynamics and sometimes it is the reverse. This is true even in the third case, in which the explanation as well as the anticipation are correct, for example, the equality of the angles of incidence and of reflection explained by the action of the ball and the reaction of the wall.

In the third case, we can also maintain that the whole geometry of directions could be deduced from dynamics,[1] namely, that the symmetry of the preceding angles depends on that of actions and reactions. The horizontality of water depends on its weight. The rotations and displacements of the rods, or of the thin pieces of wood, depend on the relationships between the push and the resistance in the two kinds of interactions that exist between the active and passive mobiles and between the mobiles and the support on which they rest, whence the necessity for coordinating two distinct systems of references, etc. If this is the case, it is clear that the spatial operations of displacement, direction, etc., become explanatory only when consonant with dynamics and "attributed" to objects, since these determine, in their causal connections, the geometric relationships isomorphic with those appropriate to our operations. Needless to say, the causal interpretation is possible only if the shapes and initial position of the objects are given, that is, by granting them spatial as well as kinetic and dynamic properties.

This close interdependence of the physical geometry of the objects, isomorphic to that of the subject, and of their dynamics can, moreover, be detected beginning with the most elementary concepts. For the child who arrives at these concepts, a straight line, for example, is geometrically such that each of its segments can coincide with any other of the same length, if laid on top of it, provided that it goes forward and that it is not brought back to the point of departure as on a circumference. From the point of

---

[1] In a way comparable to what the subject does when he makes up his own geometry by means of operations stemming from actions themselves, all of which include kinematics and even dynamics.

view of kinetics or dynamics, moreover, it is characteristic of the trajectories, which follow each other without changing directions. If, in the first of these two cases, it is the subject who constructs the straight line, a logico-mathematical operation that can be applied to the object, then in the second case it is the objects, although they thus resume the properties inherent in the first of these constructions and therefore constitute geometric as well as dynamic operational agents. At the extreme limits of our knowledge, when the theory of relativity reduces the movement of stars to inertial movements that nevertheless obey the laws of curvatures of space, we can see in it a total geometrization of celestial mechanics. However, since these curvatures themselves depend on masses, according to Einstein, we find again the interdependence of dynamics and spatial structure.[2]

In addition to the preceding genetic examples, a striking case of this interaction is the conservation of the dimensions of mobiles which leaves invariant the group of displacements. Indeed, it is not until level IIB (age 9 to 10) that the subject, having noted by congruence the equality of the lengths of two rulers, admits that they remain equal when one of them is moved forward a little and extends beyond the other by about half its length. Until this point the child considers the one that was pushed as having become longer, because of the piece extending beyond the other. When

[2] It is true that in the last 20 years we have seen attempts at a total reduction of dynamics to geometry, fields and bodies being no longer conceived as entities plunged *into* space, which they no longer are, according to Einstein, or interacting with it, but as parts or forms *of* space, without any other existence than the spatial. However, on the one hand, we must not forget the existence of life and, if the macromolecules that make up organisms are only spatial, this space will finally be enriched by an impressive number of new properties rather close to a system of "actions." On the other hand, as long as we make the distinction between the geometric operations of the subject and the space-time objective of the "environment" (and biology forces us to do this), we shall, in this sense, be able to speak of a space of objects, even if these objects are only the loci of spatio-temporal transformations. Then we shall find again between these objective transformations and the operations of the subject the same relationship as between causality as a production of shapes and movements, since this space is spatio-temporal, and operational structures as intemporal productions. (See also Part Two.)

the subject is asked about this extension, it is considered to be longer than the opposite extension of the other ruler. We can sum up this situation by saying that, up to and including level IIA, the subject does not sufficiently differentiate between displacements and extensions. We shall see in §12 that, in the case of elastics or springs (R54), their stretching is taken for a kind of displacement by virtue of the same lack of differentiation. Moreover, this extension of the mobiles, assumed in the case of the rulers and real in the case of the elastics, is not thought to be evenly distributed but to have a higher coefficient toward the front, this factor becoming identical with that of the ordinal estimates: longer equals reaching farther. What is interesting about these reactions and about their disappearance or decrease at level IIB, that is, the appearance of conservation of the length of the rulers and a beginning understanding of the expansion of the elastic, is that this apparently purely geometric evolution is closely linked to that of dynamics itself. We shall see in §10 that movement is seen at level IIA as constituting a force by itself, whereas at level IIB, force and movement are differentiated, the former being considered the cause of the latter. We then see the kinship of these two kinds of developments. As long as the movement itself remains dynamic, the mobile is provided with a kind of "internal motor," in addition to its external motor, both in a quasi-Aristotelian sense. This power is expressed by an undifferentiated concept depending at the same time on the displacement and on the forward extension, even though, from the point of view of geometry, these are not put in reference with an immobile system of external coordinates, since the only references consist of the objects which the mobile goes beyond, including the external motor, or of a kind of autoreference between one state and the next. At level IIB, when the force is differentiated from the movement, the external motor is sufficient to explain the latter, which is reduced in this case to a simple displacement: In geometric terms the displacement is put in reference with an immobile and external system of coordinates, developed accurately at about age 9 to 10, as was demonstrated by the preceding example of the horizontality of water or by the fact that the sloping objects fall vertically and no longer along the line extending from and determined by their slope, etc. In short, the invariance of lengths, the differentiation of displacements, the interfigural references, etc., are established in connection with the differentiation of forces and of movements, the progress in the understanding of the two areas of geometry and dynamics depending on both.

All things considered, the logico-geometric operations can therefore be attributed to the object in a manner comparable to what we have observed in transitivity, in reversible compensations, or in additive compositions, and therefore in the most general logico-mathematical operations, but with one fundamental difference: In this case, only two systems are present, the operations of the subject and the operating agents which are objects, isomorphic with the first but enriched by a dynamic significance. In the case of spatial operations, on the other hand, there are three systems: the purely spatial geometry of the subject, the spatio-temporal geometry of the object, and its dynamics. We have just been led to admit that, when it comes to objects, and therefore to attributed operations, the spatial operational agents and the dynamics are interdependent. But we still must consider whether the development of the geometric operations of the subject precedes his geometrico-dynamic causal explanations, and therefore whether the applied spatial operations precede the attributions, or whether there is action in both directions as there was in the situation examined in §§ 4–8. In the final analysis, it is a question of knowing whether the reflexive abstraction remains necessary to the whole of this vast tripartite construction, as it is in the cases previously analyzed, even with the possibility of being functionally stimulated by the action of contents stemming from simple abstraction, or whether the simple physical abstraction suffices for all needs.

Indeed, when the child discovers that the level of water is horizontal because it is heavy and that, on an incline, the higher parts would exert their weight and come down, he must then be in possession of the necessary operations to build a system of coordinates and to understand the opposition of vertical and horizontal directions. But if the construction of such a system is achieved at about age 9, the average age of causal explanations, because of the generalization of the operations involving measures in two or three dimensions, must we admit that there was at first the geometric construction and only then its applications and attributions to the physical process, or that the first took place at the time of a series of physical and causal problems, the last of which furnishes us with one example among many possible ones? Likewise, at about age 11 to 12, when the subject becomes capable of coordinating rotations and displacements, taking into account two systems of references at the same time, it is clear that, without this last ability, linked to formal operations or operations on operations (group INRC, etc.), he would not be able to solve his causal problem. But here again, were there at first logico-geometric operations and then applications followed by attributions, or were there correlative constructions prompted by the physical problem but carried out by reflexive abstractions?

In these cases, a regular order of succession or of priorities hardly seems likely from the very fact that there are, consistently and at all levels, three systems, the geometry of the subject, that of the object, and dynamics. Indeed, simple abstraction stemming from observation is not sufficient to engender operational transformations, even if the geometry of the object already provides forms and thus favors the construction by the subject of forms that are similar but that suggest many others, thanks to the power of transformations. Likewise, it seems clear that, if the totality of the laws furnished by the experiment in a given field is not sufficient to the construction of a causal explanation without the construction of an operational apparatus to provide a reason for it, it nevertheless gives rise to this construction through the needs it brings about, that is, by creating a desire. In fact, in this case, as in all cases, a desire is already a semicompetence, because the sensitivity to a problem is felt only when the instruments necessary to its solution are sought. In short, in the field of spatial operations, even more than in the others, because of the trilogy we have just discussed, the physical content constantly stimulates the construction of operational forms since it already includes geometric forms that will be inserted, when realized, within the system of possible forms that go beyond them while integrating them.

10. The Composition of Forces

Having first examined the additive components and then the problems of directions, we are now ready to consider the composition of the forces that derive simultaneously from both, since the forces depend on masses that can be added arithmetically, and, if not on masses, on accelerations (but not before stage III) or at least on velocities, both of which have directions. But before examining these components, let us first review the evolution of the idea of force and its progressive differentiation beginning with the action.

In the first place, let us note that a complex idea such as $f = ma$ can result either from a synthesis of initially distinct components, as is the case of weight and volume insofar as they are components of density, or from differentiations and progressive coordinations, starting with the simplest, undifferentiated ideas, as is the case in the kinematics of the velocity ratio $v = e/t$ starting with velocity overtaking. We shall see the reasons for adopting this second solution in the case of force, starting with the dimension "action" [1] or spatio-temporal thrust and going through a step we can formulate as $fte = mve$ (therefore, $\left[\dfrac{d(my)}{dt}\right]^{te}$ but not yet mdv equivalent to ma, which is glimpsed only in stage III).[2]

---

[1] In fact, the physical dimension "action" A is defined as being the product of energy E and time t, therefore, $A = E \cdot t$, which amounts to $A = Fe \cdot t$ because energy is measured by the work Fe, where F = force and e = the distance covered. It follows that the action is also equivalent to $A = Ft \cdot e$, where Ft is the "impulse." On the other hand, from $A = \frac{1}{2}mv^2 \cdot t$ we deduce $A = \frac{1}{2}mv \cdot e$, since $v = e/t$, and, being satisfied with the *vis viva* of Leibniz' mv^2, we have $A = mv \cdot e$, that is, the momentum, $p = mv$, times the space covered. It is this spatio-temporal momentum, *mvte*, that seems to constitute the initial undifferentiated idea, without a synthesis of previous and distinct ideas, *m, v,* and *e*. More precisely, the undifferentiated kinetic idea *v* is completed when it intervenes in a dynamic interpretation (at level IIA, when force is confused with movement itself) through a global link with the weight of the object, *m,* and the more or less long space that it covers, *e.*

[2] We must recall that Newton himself wrote his second law in the form $f = d(mv)/dt$. The forms $f = ma$ or $f = m\, dv/dt$ are really Euler's and not

Insofar as the idea of force derives from the undifferentiated concept of "action," it therefore does not correspond to a particular operation of the subject, which would be attributed in its specificity to the object, but rather to general powers ascribed to reality by analogy with those of the action itself. It is then their progressive compositions that will, by successive attributions, move more and more toward operational forms. As for the convergence of the forces at work in reality and those that intervene in the conduct of the subject, they are taken for granted as long as material actions are involved.[3]

Let us therefore try to retrace the steps in the formation of this concept of action or of force in the light of R41 and of the beginnings of R42 and to relate them to those that have been indicated (§ 9) for the directions:

> R41 deals with contiguous marbles hung by strings from a horizontal rod. A swinging of the first and its impact on the second set the last in motion by a transmission analogous to those of R2. At level IA, the emphasis is on the powers of the active marble, sometimes with mention of speeds and even weights, which are, however, undifferentiated at the core of an "action" still close to the action itself. In R42 we posed two kinds of problems: first, the comparison

Newton's, in a corollary of Euler's mechanics in the form of $m = f/a$. The best current texts go back to Newton's original formula, which can be generalized in relativistic mechanics, where mass is not conserved.

[3] Even in the area of purely deductive or formal operations, we can perceive the following analogies, which seem to include some truth despite their bold character. To the spatio-temporal momentum $p = mv$ would correspond any operational action the power of which is dependent on (1) the quantity of manipulated elements, by extension, field of operation, which would correspond to m; (2) the operational path they are made to cover in one stroke, for example, in a recursive procedure, that would correspond to v. Having accepted this, the operational correspondent of $d(mv)$ would then be a modification of the operation, for example, in the direction of what can be called, since Goedel, a "stronger" structure, that is, having available more "powerful" synthetic instruments. For example, one can reasonably maintain that a reasoning by recurrence [recurrence: process of reasoning that consists in extending to all terms in a series what is valid for the first two.— *Trans.*] is "stronger" than a series of syllogisms by themselves alone, because at the time it concerns an unlimited series of elements and because its procedure is more rapid.

between the "efforts," etc., made respectively by two people, one
making a detour from A to B without carrying a pack and another
traveling along the straight line AB but with a pack, and second,
the comparison between the propulsion by impact of a mobile from
A to B and its moving by being pushed along the same path. To
these two problems the subjects of level IA respond by alternatively
calling on one or the other of the factors involved without succeeding in confronting them. If the central concept at level IA is really
that of the spatio-temporal action of a push, etc., we cannot yet assimilate it with the physical dimension "action" because it remains
essentially psycho- or biomorphic.

At level IB we observe noticeable beginnings of decentration. For
the suspended marbles, the subjects stress more the kinetic factors
and the weights, but without conservation, and conceive of a succession of actions in the form of a chain reaction of immediate
external transmissions (cf. § 4). To the problems of R42 they
respond by a qualitative equivalence between the forces expended
for a straight run with a pack and a detour without it, but they fail
to understand thrust and pull. As for the directions, we are re-
minded of the beginning of rotation, when the passive object is not
pushed in the middle. We can then talk of going from the psychomorphic action to the bare beginnings of the action with a physical
significance.

At level IIA when, as we recall, we see the beginning of semi-
internal mediate transmissions (§ 4) and of a series of progressive
steps in the anticipation of directions when the impacts or thrusts
are not direct hits, the results of R42 show that on the horizontal
plane the subjects judge that the forces necessary to propel an
object by means of a blow or by pushing it step by step for the
same distance are equal. In R41 the emphasis is on the speeds and
their changes, that is, impetus at take-off [*prise de l'élan*],* so that
we can already talk about a kind of "force" in the sense of dp.
However, an important distinction is observed when we come to the
reactions of levels IIA and IIB. In IIA, this force or *élan* stays inside the movement, in the sense that the movement or the speed
constitutes by itself the force,[4] which we can write as *fte = pe,*

* *Translator's note: Prise de l'élan:* gathering up of forces previous to a
take-off.

[4] Let us note in this respect that this concept of movement and speed as
forces was retained in the history of physics, at least sporadically, until
rather recently, and is found again in certain manuals for centrifugal

where $p = mv$. In IIB, however, the force is differentiated from it and represents the cause of the movement or of its changes, hence $f \rightarrow dp$. In Polish, which has two different words for *élan,* either high speed or "impetus at take-off" [*prise de l'élan*], the children questioned by A. Szeminska change their terminology significantly in this respect.

Level IIB shows marked progress in solving the problems of directions, without doubt in relation to this more advanced differentiation between dynamics and kinematics. This progress consists of attempts at coordinations between rotations and translations or at covariations between angles of incidence and reflection, etc. (see § 9). However, the fact that force becomes the cause of the movement, while pushing the subject to face a series of new dynamic problems, leads him by that very fact to certain apparent regressions. For example, because weight produces various effects and especially plays a role in the makeup of the vertical, or of the horizontality of water, etc., its action is no longer conserved in accordance with its placement. The weight increases with the thrust or when it is placed near the bottom, and it often decreases with speed, which we can write as $m = p/v$.

Finally, in stage III, the subjects of R41 admit that there is a regular acceleration of marbles on the downgrade, while the difficulties noted at level IIB disappear. We can therefore speak of a beginning of the force $f = ma$.

These results are found again in an analogous study (R43) in which, with the tracks banked on both sides, the marble goes up the opposite slope and goes down again, etc. In stage I the heights reached have no connection with those of the starting points. At level IIA the anticipations are better, but with a focus on the length of the slope and not yet on the height. At level IIB the height intervenes in the course of the observations, but since some subjects think that the speed diminishes with the descent, they are at first very much surprised by the opposite result. In stage III, finally, the role of height is foreseen from the outset and, in addition to acceleration, we can note some progress in the concept of force. The equivalence in the heights of the points of arrival and the points of departure make some subjects say that "the thrust is necessary" or speak of a "suspended force," which brings to mind the idea of

"force"—giving rise to the critical remarks of Hertz, for whom a force has meaning only when "present *before* the movement" (*The Principles of Mechanics,* Dover, p. 6).

energy but which is as yet only the generalization of the idea formed at this stage, namely, that forces continue to exist in the immobile state.

The evolution of the idea of force is therefore rather peculiar in that it does not come from a synthesis of previous elements but from a differentiation and coordination of characteristics that were initially undifferentiated. Indeed, the subject does not start out with an idea of mass that would be given independently of force by a simple composition of quantities of matter, nor with an idea of a movement with its speed, without reference to forces, in order to synthesize mass and movement into a new idea. On the contrary, in the beginning stages, mass already possesses a force, as movement does by itself, and it is only later, once they are differentiated, that they can be coordinated in what may be called a synthesis.

To begin with mass, the child at first speaks only of "bigness" and of weight. For us, weight is obviously a force, in the precise sense of a mass linked to the acceleration of the attraction of the earth. However, for young subjects this acceleration does not play a role and we could believe that what the child calls weight is only a quantity of matter, and therefore mass. But according to these children, this weight exercises all kinds of actions stemming from force and going in all kinds of directions. A heavy pebble dropped into a glass of water drags the water down toward the bottom or pushes it up to the top without regard to its volume. A ball with a hole in it, which fills with water on its way down, will likewise push up the level because it becomes heavy. The same holds true for a large tube with three holes at different heights, the highest of which will produce the largest jet of water because there is more water underneath it, and the water exerts its pressure in rising as well as in falling, etc. In short, weight is at first a force with quantity and action undifferentiated, and therefore a sort of coefficient of action. We have seen that up to level IIA the same applies to movement, which is force as much as speed and displacement.

When these ideas are sufficiently differentiated, a synthesis takes place between the additive components applicable to weight considered as mass, and the ordinal operations that constitute speed. In § 11 we shall discuss this operational synthesis, which is attributed to objects at the same time as it is the source of vectoral components of forces. But let us remember that such syntheses of ideas that have now become clear but were at first scarcely differentiated are encountered in the purely operational realm. It is thus that the whole number is conceived at age 7 to 8 by a synthesis of classes and the order inherent in relationships that can be seriated, while at the preoperational levels the figurate numbers, the figural collections, and the beginnings of seriation all have some characteristics borrowed simultaneously from what will later become numbers, classes, and seriations. But the synthesis of force, although analogous in form (additions and order) comes later because it apparently happens only at the time of compositions we shall now discuss.

11. The Components of Forces and the Constitution of Vectors

The criterion for establishing the fact that the formation of an operator is completed is assuredly the subject's capacity for compositions, the progressive constitution of which undoubtedly plays the decisive role in this formation, because a force in the operational sense exists only in collaboration with, or in opposition to, others. This is what we must now examine.

In a preliminary research (R44) we placed three weights, F_1, F_2, and F_3, so that they hung by means of pulleys on three sides of a square tray and pulled on a mobile indicator placed in the center, with a simple match placed at the interesection of the strings. At level IA the child does not figure out that, if we add a weight to one of the three directions, the indicator will move in the direction of this weight. It can go in any direction, as if the added weight were repelling it or deflecting it; or again, it cannot move because it is "too heavy," that is, it can hold itself back. On the other hand, on observation, traction is understood. Later, when two equal weights are added to F_1 and F_2, with F_3 remaining unchanged, the match will be pulled not along the median but first toward one and then toward the other, because the forces operate only in motion and do not work together, which perhaps results from a like principle of individual autonomous action. Of course, these subjects can neither explain the balance nor understand why it does not change with equal additions to the three weights. At level IB the subjects understand that an addition will move the index toward the increased weight, but they cannot predict the result of two equal additions. They think that either the indicator will not move, as in the case of two equal weights opposite each other and therefore without any concern for directions, or else that there is a choice, on one side *or* the other, or that there is an alternation as in level IA. At stage II (37% at age 6 to 7, 71% at age 8 to 9, and 66% at age 10 to 12) the problem of the resulting median for two equal increases on the three forces is resolved but, as soon as it is a question of different variations of the three components, the composition becomes impossible. There is then a return to the preoperational reactions of the IB type, and we have to wait until stage II, about age 11 to 12, to find an intuition of the exact directions.

R45 deals with other preliminary problems. Two weights, *A* and *A'*, pull in opposite directions the same string stretched horizontally on two pulleys attached to a vertical wall. Then we hang in the middle of this string a third weight *B,* the effects of which will then have to be predicted and explained, once the connections between *A* and *A'* are understood. The relationships themselves are poorly understood in stage I, in connection with what we saw in § 6. At level IA the subject does not even know what is going to go up or go down in this M-shaped setup. At level IB he knows that one of the two weights, *A* or *A'*, holds the other back, but without any concern for quantification. To hold back in *A* a weight of 50 g, a subject of 4;9 puts in *A'* a little toy weighing about 5 g. When $A = 1$, $B = 0$, and $A' = 1$, a subject of 6;6 says that it is *A* that "pulls taut" the most because it was placed last (in time). Another subject, who was 6 years old, in comparing $B = 2$ to $A = 1$ and $A' = 1$, thinks that $B > (A + A')$ because each of the *A*'s is by itself, etc. But the clearest manifestation of the lack of quantitative composition peculiar to this stage is that when we load *A* and *A'* at the expense of *B*, not only will the string *AA'* go through a horizontal level but also, when we proceed further, *B* will go above the line *AA'* and with its string will form a rooflike shape—for example, when *A* and $A' = 8$, weights of 50 g each, and $B = 2$ weights! In stage II, this abnormal ascent ends, but already when

$A = B = A'$ and *a fortiori* when B is lighter than A or A', the line AA' is still often predicted to be horizontal because B "no longer weighs anything." With this exception, there are certainly compensations between A and A', as we have seen in § 6, but the balance is explained by the fact that a weight can no longer pull when others hold it back, which is the same thing as saying that a weight cannot pull and hold back at the same time. At rest, the weights "no longer do anything, all they do is hold the string" (7;7), or again, "When it moves it pulls, when it does not move, it is taut" (9;0). In stage III, finally, the three new developments are the bipolarity of functions, that is, each weight is pulled at the same time that it pulls and is held back at the same time that it holds back, the resulting reciprocity being extended to the whole system—"because they all pull" (10;2), or "there is no direction" (12;3), but a general interaction—and the fact that the force continues to act on the immobile state.

The lack of sufficient quantification in stages I and sometimes even II, which plays an essential role in the difficulties of composition, was analyzed in R46 and 47. The problem in these two studies was one of weights either suspended one beneath the other at varying intervals, or in parallel columns, or hooked on, some horizontally and others vertically, etc. The purpose was to determine their equivalent or different effects, with objective equality of weights, either when they are placed on the same side of a tray where the strings tying them together pull an elastic (R46), or when they are on opposite sides of the tray and therefore in a state of balance (R47). The two kinds of results completely converged, but one was controlled by means of the other because of the complexity of the observed evolution. In stage I there is no additivity because, for obviously psychomorphic reasons, the action of weight is a complex one in which the force in question depends not only on the weights but also on the strings and their lengths, on the height of the columns, on the positions, etc.—in short, on a whole context recalling that of the action itself. That is particularly the case when it comes to the way in which one weight is hooked to another, which leads to common efforts that are more powerful than the sum of the individual actions, etc. A subject who is 6;10 goes as far as saying that the string F, being less heavy than each weight P, can decrease the sum total, whence $(3P + F) < (3P)$, since $F < P$! For other subjects, a long string helps the traction. At level IIA there is a strict additivity, independent of the positions and in terms of the number of weights alone, according to the process of compensation and reversibility described in § 6. On the other hand, at level IIB, where, as we have seen in § 10, the idea of force is differentiated from movements and speeds to become their cause, this dynamic progress carries with it an apparent regression to nonadditivity although for very different reasons than in stage I. For example, the nature of weight being to pull downwards, its force will increase near the bottom in a vertical column and will decrease when in a horizontal position, etc. Finally, in stage III, there is a return to additivity, but in a dynamic sense: "They form a whole and they pull in the same way." In adding up the results of R46 and 47 in addition to those of R48, where weights that are piled up or distributed in different ways on a tray push a rod down into a soft support, we find, for these four levels, 86% of the subjects belonging to stage I from age 4 to 6, 78% in level IIA from age 7 to 8, 73% of IIB from age 9 to 10, and 61% of stage III from age 11 to 12.

Since the other obstacle to composition is the modification of forces according to whether there is movement or rest, we should recall R19. Up to and including level IIA, it takes more force to keep a cart immobile on a slope than to make it climb. Indeed, as long as we hold it back, there is a tendency for it to roll down, whereas if we pull it up, it no longer goes down and, this downward tendency being eliminated, a lesser force is needed.

Finally, let us come to the very laws of composition in accordance with the intensities and directions of forces. In R49, weights that can be placed in a semicircle are put in twos at 0–0° (parallel), then at 90–90° (opposite each other), and then at 30–30° and 60–60°; each set pulls on an elastic fastened to a hook in the center. Other variations have confirmed the results obtained. In level IA there are no correct anticipations. In level IB the subject understands that, if the weights pull at their maximum at 0–0° and are immobilized at 90–90°, the effects will decrease in going from 0–0° to 30–30° and then to 60–60°. But the angles are not considered, and the only factors remembered are the length of the strings between the pulleys and the elastic, the length of which varies according to its stretching, or the distances in relation to the free end of the elastic or to the hook. In stage II the angle is noted and described, but its action is not understood. The subject does not go beyond the factors of lengths of the strings or distance. It is not until stage III (age 11 to 12) that the child explains the decrease in the action of weights by the fact that they pull on different sides and its increase when they come closer together, and that he therefore realizes the role of the directions and of the angle.

R17, already cited in § 6, demonstrates it in a systematic way. The apparatus is circular, with movable pulleys along the circumference. In the first part (I), two weights are placed at various angles and the problem is to find the weight that will put them in balance when it is placed opposite the resultant of the first two. In the second part (II), the positions of the first two weights are fixed at 60° and 90°, but their values vary; the problem is to find the direction of the one opposite their resultant. In case (I), therefore, the intensity to be found in F_3 depends on the direction of the given forces F_1 and F_2, while in case (II) the direction of F_3 depends on the intensity of F_1 and F_2. In fact, the two evolutions are somewhat parallel, with sometimes a slight advantage when it comes to directions. In stage I there is failure in all problems, including case (I), in which F_1 and F_2 are at 0° and $F_3 = F_1 + F_2$, and case (II), in which $F_1 = F_2$ and the direction of F_3 is the median. At stage II (age 7 to 10), there is success in the solution of these two problems but failure in case (I) as soon as the angle increases and in case (II) as soon as the weights of F_1 and F_2 are made unequal. In this last case we observe three kinds of solutions. The subject chooses either the one opposite the bisector or median, as if the weights were equal, or he chooses the one opposite the greatest weight to neutralize it—as if that were the same as "helping the little one," as several subjects put it—or the area around the one opposite the lightest weight, which amounts again to helping it but by counterbalancing the big one instead of canceling it. Finally, in stage III, all the problems are solved through the coordination of directions and intensities. In R50 we again took up the same problems by facilitating their solutions through directed manipulations in a situation where the three weights are equal and at equal distances from each other and where the subject can vary the intensities and directions. In stage I there was no progress except where a preliminary problem was concerned: two equal and opposite forces. On the other hand, some intermediate subjects between levels I (IB) and II come closer to that progress, as a result of the exercise. In stage II we see partial progress in case (I) problems without progress in case (II) problems, or progress in case (II) problems without progress in case (I) problems, but in no case is there stable coordination between directions and intensities. Finally, some sub-

jects who were intermediate between stages II and III in the pre-test
went on to stage III but with some instability and some partial regressions in the post-test. Both R51 and 52, carried out by V. Bang,
furnish useful complements to these facts by making the comparisons between elastics in different situations, particularly in the form
of a sling in which the aiming at the target and the shooting of the
projectile visibly depend on angles. The spontaneous attitude in
stage I consists of placing the strings farther behind, even with a
more obtuse angle ($\vee$as against V), in order to shoot farther.
Some subjects predict even at age 7 "farther because farther apart"
before noting "farther because tighter." None of the young subjects
thinks on his own of closing the angle. When the components are
unequal (i.e., one string is longer than the other), the initial attitude
is to pull "harder." In the case of two elastics joined in a parallel
line (A and A_1) followed by a single elastic B in stage I, it is B
that has the most force because it stretches more and, even at level
IIA, the subject at first predicts that, by pulling the whole thing,
the index separating A and A' from B will remain "toward the
middle because they are the same size" without taking numbers into
account. However, while in stage I the force is confined only to
the side where it is being pulled, starting with stage II a distinction
is made between the forces of stretching and resistance. If we come
back to the sling, by putting on one side two parallel elastics A and
A' and on the other a single B of the same length, the subjects of
stage I do not go beyond the symmetry, "it goes straight," and we
have to wait until level IIB (age 9 to 10) before the inequality
raises a problem at the time of prediction and not just after observation. It is not until stage III that the problem is solved, especially if
we oppose to the parallels A and A' an elastic B of double length.
In short, the technics of elastics pulled by hand, and especially in
the case of the sling, do not result in aiding understanding, which
we could have expected, and gives results that fall into the same
stages as the ones of weights suspended by strings or of elastics
pulled by weights.

The general characteristics of these compositions, as opposed to
their specifically vectoral properties, correspond in a striking manner to those of operational compositions in their common forms,
and especially to compositions of spatial relationships. The original
idea (stage I) is that each force exists individually and autono-
mously, without any relation to the others, as if it were a question
of actions not yet operational, the properties of which depend on

no system, no classification, nor any group or relations, therefore on actions that can be carried out independently of each other, and only in terms of their own conditions, such as positions, etc. In stage II, on the other hand, there is a beginning of compositions: additivity at level IIA, compensations by opposite positions, and the median resultant by symmetry for two equal divergent forces. But these compositions, dictated by the most general operational regularities, stop there; the subject understands neither the weakening of effects when equal forces diverge, nor the direction of the resultants when they are unequal. The reason for the lack of comprehension of such simple relationships is once again that the forces have not yet been put in relative positions in the form of grouped operations and remain, except for the most elementary compositions, in the state of actions taking place by themselves with their own functions, in the sense of preoperational component functions. Actually, in stage II, a weight is not supposed to be able to pull and be pulled at the same time, or to hold back or be held back, etc. Moreover, the action ceases to exist outside its own motor or kinematic development, when an operation continues to play its role even though annulled or compensated by others. Indeed, to compose two forces is to suppose at the same time that each continues to act as though it were the only one in question, and that their interaction leads to a result different from that of either taken by itself alone. Therein lies precisely the secret of operational compositions as opposed to actions or to preoperational functions expressing their dependencies only when there is actual change or variation. There is therefore a remarkable parallel between the development of operational compositions in general and that of the compositions of forces. That is how the latter play the role of operations attributed to objects. We shall return to this in connection with stage III and with strictly vectoral compositions.

But two remarks are in order. First of all, we now see why the construction of force by synthesis (§ 10) could be completed only in terms of the compositions of that force. In fact, they are the only ones able to reach that point, which frees this concept of force from its ties with the undifferentiated characteristics of the action, the limitations of which assert themselves in level IIB, and which, in stage III, really make it an operation or operator.

On the other hand, we shall note the rather close relationships between the stages of this composition of forces and what we saw in § 9 relating to the directions of movements following thrusts, tractions, or impacts, and therefore to directions not of forces but of movements that come from them. We observed in stage I the prime importance of the direction of the projector, the passive object being forced to take that direction without any consideration of the point of impact. Therefore, we again encounter the initial idea of an independence of the active force that need not take into account conditions other than its own. Then we observe a progressive differentiation of directions, first without coordination of rotations and translations, then with progress in level IIB at the time of the construction of a system of references. It is only in stage III that the problems are solved by the simultaneous consideration of two systems of reference and by relationships of action and reaction.

Therefore, we have yet to solve the problem of understanding why we must wait until stage III for the subject to achieve vectoral compositions as elementary as that of finding the resultant of two unequal and divergent forces. Let us recall first that the utilization of diagonals is implicitly understood at the outset of stage II with the construction of double-entry tables or matrices, and it is explicitly understood in level IIB with the systems of natural coordinates. In level IIA the subject spontaneously succeeds in constructing a two-dimensional matrix to express the Cartesian product of two groups of relationships. For example, to arrange leaves according to their sizes and colors from light to dark, he will construct a double-entry table so that the sizes are seriated from left to right and the colors from top to bottom. In this case the relationship between two leaves, one of which is both larger and darker than the other, is read diagonally or according to an oblique line connecting two squares belonging neither to the same column nor to the same row. When it is a question of spatial directions in a rectangular system of coordinates, it is *a fortiori* the same thing; therefore, the subject finds without any difficulty an intermediate direction between two others when these are divergent.

Moreover, in the usual graphic representation of vectors there intervenes a rule that would seem irrelevant, since we in no way ask the subjects of our experiments to refer to it, nor especially to use anything learned in school. They are to represent a force of greater intensity by a line whose length is proportional to it. Now, there is much more than a rule involved in this. In order to compare directions and intensities, it is necessary to find not only a common language but also homogeneous properties. In this case, if the direction answers the question "where is the object going?" when displaced by the force, for example the indicator pulled by the weight of R44 or R17, the intensity corresponds to the question "where does it stop?" The fundamental operation of the addition of two vectors ($\oplus$), as opposed to scalar or numerical addition ($+$), therefore consists of: (1) representing the *distances covered* by the mobiles animated by each of the two forces as if it were the only one in question; (2) imagining these distances covered with their two inseparable characteristics of direction and length; (3) placing them end to end, $\angle$ in $\sim$ or $\sim$ connecting the two extremities (big diagonal), or more simply connecting their extremities, $\triangle$, taking for the resultant the median point of this little diagonal; in other words, bringing together the two distances covered into one, taking into account their lengths and not only their directions.

Thus, immediately see that the constitution and the composition of vectors present the same central character as those of operations in general, as we said above in opposing the composition of forces to that of any actions, and that is to consider each component as continuing to act with its own properties, all the while being integrated into a whole, the properties of which are new and different. Even though it is easy to understand that 5 and 7 are always present [1] within 12 in an addition such as $5 + 7 = 12$, it is much more difficult when two distances covered produce a third that no longer has either the same lengths or the same directions as those of the components!

It is at this point that we need to have recourse to the formal operations of stage III and that we can consider the compositions of forces or of vectors as formal operations attributed to the objects

---

[1] It is, on the other hand, less easy to understand why, if 5 and 7 are prime numbers, 12 is divisible by 2, 3, 4, and 6, whence the synthetic character of this operation, like that of causality, which Kant was not so wrong in maintaining.

themselves. The first characteristic of these hypothetico-deductive operations is the ability to deal with the possible, which permits us, in a particular case, to consider simultaneously a force acting as it would when isolated and when modified by interaction with others, or when continuing to act while at rest, or when capable of covering a certain distance even if it does not actually do it. This "possible" is clearly physical in character and not only concerns the hypotheses of the subject when his assumptions have yet to be checked, but also intervenes in the "possible constructions" of states of equilibrium as it does in all composition. In the second place, formal operations are operations on operations and do not remain at the first power; this is already the case of force when it becomes synthesis and it is the case *a fortiori* of preceding compositions. In the third place, formal operations comprise a combinatory and a quaternity. The vectors presuppose a "totality of parts" with it combinatory nature, and the coordination of two systems of reference implies a quaternity, without naturally speaking of the group and of the body both of which characterize vectoral space about which many other psychogenetic studies could be made. Briefly, the most general characteristics of formal operations are all found again in these compositions by virtue of transformations executed by the objects and not only applied to them by the subject.

12. Linearity, Proportionality, and Distributivity

In connection with transitivity and transmissions (§§ 4–5), compensations or reversibility (§ 6), additive compositions (§§ 7–8), and spatial operations (§ 9), we saw that we could detect a double progression in the development of these fundamental operational structures. First, there is progress in attribution, on the one hand, which permits the subject, once he has worked out his operations as a result of reflexive abstractions, to find them again in the objects in order to submit these to his causal explanations. Reciprocally, from the formative stages on, there is a group of influences of causality on the subject, to the extent that his experience

of objects furnishes him with a set of contents favoring this operational structuring. Obviously, such a double process, if it is general,
must be found again in connection with the compositions of forces,
but in §§ 10 and 11 we insisted only on the aspect of attribution
because at first glance we could hardly see how these compositions,
visibly copied from algebraic-numerical and geometric structures
from which vectoral space is derived, could contribute to the
spontaneous development of big operational structures. However,
when we recall the essential roles of linearity and particularly of
proportions and of distributivity constantly at work in the play of
vectors, it is only on them that the preceding question must be
focused, resulting in the following two problems: First, are these
eminently logico-mathematical structures really found again in the
properties of objects, or do they only constitute operations applied
by the subject to facilitate his figuring? Second, if they are effectively attributed, what is the possible contribution of proportions
and physical distributivities in the psychogenetic construction of
these operational *schèmes* which are in other respects geometric,
algebraic, and logical?

Beginning with proportions, a number of former studies showed
that in all these fields quantitative proportionality is reached only in
stage III, beginning with a qualitative form necessary to the comprehension of the equivalence of the two relationships and permitting
a subsequent quantification, which then intervenes more or less
rapidly. We were therefore interested in finding out whether in a
linear composition of vectors, such as the multiplication of vectors
involved in a state of equilibrium by a same scalar preserving the
equilibrium, at least a qualitative understanding would be more
precocious or whether it would always be at the same level. R53
answered this question. In a vertical apparatus where two unequal
weights $x > y$ move an elastic in given direction, the subject is
simply asked, after having modified x, what must be added to y to
keep the same direction. At stage I there is no solution. At level
IIA the subject adds equal weights, as if by equalizing the adjunctions x' and y' nothing will be modified, or he even manages to obtain a final equalization $(x + x') = (y + y')$ to prevent the elastic
from greater deviation. Starting with level IIB, we observe as usual
intermediary behaviors testifying to a beginning of a feeling for
proportionality but leading to constructions that are simply additive.

As soon as we have $x > y$, the subject adds more weight to x than to y, but without looking for the double or the triple in x according to whether $y' = y$ or $2y$. Or again he confines himself to equal adjunctions, but with the relational intention of "keeping the same difference." It is only in stage III that the multiplicative composition intervenes, with reasoning underlining the discovery of the equality of relationships, "it will be the same weight but twice as much" (11;1), etc.

As for distributivity, we have studied it in two situations, one of stretching or causality peculiar to the object (R54), the other of transfer from one container to the other or causal action of the subject but ending in a composition of simple quantities of matter (R55). The stretching of an elastic offers a beautiful example of distributivity inherent in the object and easy to study by comparing the lengthenings, for example, of two successive segments a (proximal) and b (pulled to its extremity). In level IA the segment that is pulled will stretch more than the other. In IB, if $a > b$, this inequality will remain when it is pulled but in spite of and not because of this transformation: a becomes longer simply because it is already long, etc. In level IIA, with the appearance of "semi-internal" transmissions, there is added to the actions of pulling the concept of a modification of the rubber itself in such a way that if $a > b$ the adjunctions $a' > b'$ are determined by a kind of qualitative [1] correlate (b "will never catch up" with a), but still without any homogeneity; a can grow proportionately much more than b, etc. Level IIB marks the beginning of multiplicative constructions, but they still remain partially undifferentiated from additions; for example, for Ana at 9;5, the double of 6 will still be $6 + 2$, etc. This relative undifferentiation means that the stretching is itself still poorly differentiated from a displacement, as though the action of pulling amounted to the displacement of the outermost points of the segments of the elastic in addition to the dilation of the rubber itself. Finally, the subjects in stage III reach the point of postulating the homogeneity of transformations, which are then reduced to the stretching alone. If the whole is E and the parts a, b, c, etc., the initial idea is, therefore, that $T(E) = T(a) + T(b) + T(c) + \ldots$, which seems to correspond to the notion of internal mediate transmission characteristic of this level and which the subject expresses qualitatively by saying that the elastic will stretch to its whole length in the same way. It is only when he goes from the principle to the computation that the problem be-

---

[1] In Spearman's terms, a' is to a as b' is to b, but without quantification.

comes complicated by the fact that the distributivity $n(a + b) = na + nb$ is actually a play of proportions:

$$\frac{a + b}{n(a + b)} = \frac{a}{na} = \frac{b}{nb}$$

Even though a simple proportion such as $a/b:a'/b'$ is accessible from the beginnings of stage III, this distributive relationship is more complex when it comes to the proportion between the whole and the parts, in such a way that in level IIA the subject again gets to a heterogeneity of the coefficients of stretching, but for refined reasons such as the ones that the coefficient of the big segment must be superior to that of the little one, etc. It is only in level IIIB (11 to 12) that the solution is found in its apparent simplicity: "Since it stretches equally, the two parts have to double," or "there is no reason why it stretches more in one place than in another," which covers, as always, a big operational complexity.

However, if distributivity is so difficult to master in the case of the elastic, perhaps it is because, causally, the homogeneous distribution of the perturbation is not easily grasped.[2] So, it was necessary to examine the distributivity of a simple composition of quantities of liquids: to pour water into two receptacles of different shapes A and B, then to pour A and B into C, to mark C and to double its quantity, which we shall call $2C$, then to ask what will happen when the water of $2C$ goes back into A and B, or into $A + A'$ and $B + B'$, when A' and B' are glasses similar to A and B. The stages obtained correspond rather strikingly to those that have just been discussed: no coordination of transformations in stage I; additive comparisons in level IIA by direct comparisons between the quantity $2C$ and the available glasses; a beginning of multiplicative composition in IIB but with varied undifferentiations between addition and multiplication; immediate success in level IIIA for the duplication but still failure for the triple; and then general success in IIIB. We thus see that it is not the elasticity that prevented understanding of the distributivity of R54 because, although the subjects of stage I do not yet understand the conservation of the quantity of liquid transferred, which is equivalent to granting it a capacity for dilation comparable to elasticity, conservation no longer poses a problem starting with level IIA, without, however, involving distributivity.

---

[2] A control has, however, been worked out by means of springs whose stretching is due to distinct weights hung from their ends. The results obtained were the same.

Depending, of course, on the level of analysis, these facts obviously show the character of the operations validly attributed to the object assumed by linearity, distributivity, and proportionality, when set up, and in accordance with the three customary complementary meanings that we give to the term attribution when we establish it. These three meanings are (a) that it is a question of properties of objects that exist in their own right, on a certain scale, before the subject discovers them; (b) that to find them the subject needs to construct operations applicable to these objects, this construction including of necessity reflexive abstractions; (c) that, in such cases, the application does not simply consist of subjecting the objects to freely chosen structures, as is the case in applications without attributions, and, moreover, that it amounts to establishing an isomorphism between the operational structures used and the objective characteristics discovered because of them. This isomorphism thus assures an attribution and thereby furnishes the principle of an explanation that satisfies the conditions of intellectual assimilation, namely, the understanding of objects by the subject.

(a) Regarding the first of these three points,[3] what stands out in the preceding results is the increasing necessity, for the subject, because of the observed data of the experiment, to give up his initial interpretations, founded on the simple group of displacements or on the numerical additive compositions that were previously sufficient for him, in order to substitute for them models of stretching or, in general, multiplicative compositions. When the subjects in level IIA and some in IIB of R53 add equal weights to unequal weights so that nothing is changed or so that "the same difference" is maintained, they reason that the effects of weights consist of distances covered or of displacements a and b so that $a + x$ and $b + x$ keep the same divergence at the finishing points as at the starting points. In addition, in R54, when children of the same levels mainly see in the stretching of the elastic the displacement of the indicators marking the terminal boundary of the segments or of the whole, they also substitute for the concept of

[3] The following developments are due to the close collaboration of G. Henriques, R. Maier, and especially G. Cellérier, all three of whom I warmly thank.

stretching that of distances covered which can be composed by simple additions. Therefore, they have to yield to a resistance of the object when they discover in it, with the failure of their predictions, unforeseen properties that cannot be reduced to an additive composition of a spatial or numerical nature. So, in these two cases, faced by objective facts, the subjects must go beyond the models of simple displacements or of an additive group of wholes to a more refined causal model. This goes hand in hand with what we saw (§ 9) of the constant necessity of linking the geometry of the real to dynamic operators.

(b) But how does the subject go from additive compositions to multiplicative operations? The physical experience alone has never been enough to assure the construction of a multiplication. On the other hand, multiplication proceeds by reflexive abstraction, starting with addition, since to multiply x by n is to carry out n additions of x, thus $nx = (1\text{st})\ x + (2\text{nd})x \cdots + (n\text{th})x$. It is therefore a question of a recursive application of enumeration that deals not with groups of objects but with the actions themselves performed by the subject on these groups. Thus, multiplication consists of an operation on operations, therefore at the second power, resulting in delayed understanding of its real meaning as opposed to school verbalism, whether this meaning consists of attributions of multiplicative compositions to the object or of purely logico-mathematical uses. Likewise, proportions are derived by reflexive abstraction from multiplication as far as the equality of two multiplicative relations (divisions) is concerned. Finally, the distributivity $n(a + b) = na + nb$ itself rests upon the proportions $(a + b)/n(a + b):a/na:b/nb$.

(c) Then let us come to the common characteristics of the attributions included in these compositions stemming from linearity, distributivity, or simple proportionality. In general, distributivity characterizes the way in which a perturbation is distributed, and therefore the effects of an external causality, in a physical system in equilibrium, the connections and the constraints of which determine the direction of forces. Let us take as an example a situation intermediate between those of R45 and 53. Two unequal weights, a and b, are hung from pulleys fixed at the same height on a vertical wall and with a weight c tied to a horizontal string stretched between these two pulleys and therefore between a and b. In this case, the system is in equilibrium when $c = a \oplus b$. If now we add a weight c' to c, to reestablish the equilibrium it is necessary to add a' to a and b' to b in such a way as to give $c + c' = (a + a') \oplus (b + b')$ and not $a' + b' = c'$. But, since solutions by addition remain indeterminate, the general solution will be in the form $kc = ka \oplus kb$, which implies both proportionality and distributivity.

However, there is more to it than that. The vectoral space implies distributivity at several stages. In general, we can consider it as a commutative group, that of vectors, provided with operators each of which determines an automorphism of the group. The group of operators, scalars, comprises a very strong structure, that of the body, but we can limit ourselves to the group of whole numbers and be satisfied with a ring. In this case we have available a modulus instead of the whole vectoral space. Distributivity then intervenes as one of the conditions that any action or transformation must fulfill in order to be one of these operators. There are three conditions for a transformation ϕ acting on the elements of the group G of vectors: (1) that it must be an application (therefore univocal on the right); (2) that it respects the closure of G, therefore, that it transforms one vector into another without going outside the limits of the system; (3) that it be coordinated with the operation $\oplus$ of the group. In this last case, we have $\phi(a \oplus b) = \phi(a) \oplus \phi(b)$, ϕ and $\oplus$ being interchangeable.

The operator ϕ then generates an automorphism and distributivity as well as linearity, and therefore particular cases of morphism when ϕ is either ordinary multiplication or that of a vector by a scalar. It is then clear that, when the subjects of stage II mentioned above try to express the law of the stretching of the segments of the elastic by an additive composition of displacements, they do not get as far as the construction of a vectoral operator. Even though their operation satisfies conditions (1) and (2), they fail to form an automorphism because addition alone is not distributive. On the contrary, the subjects of stage III, in arriving at proportionality and distributivity, establish valid "attributions" in the field of vectoral compositions.

But we must remember the reciprocal problem. We have seen

how linearity as well as its properties of proportionality and distributivity are part of the physical property of the object, and are therefore inherent in the relationships of causality to the extent that the latter goes beyond what is observable to attain a system of necessary connections. But we have also seen how the subject succeeds in constructing by reflexive abstraction his multiplicative operations as additive operations at the second power, then his structures of proportionality by equalization of relationships (therefore, again, by relationships of relationships or relationships at the second power), and finally his structures of distributivity due to the proportions $(a + b):n(a + b) = a:na = b:nb$. It is therefore this endogenous construction of such operations that allows them to be "attributed" to the real and thus to return to certain fundamental properties of objects. But we still must ask ourselves to what point these applications accompanied by attributions have contributed to the constitution of the operations of the subject himself, at least in the last phases of development (level IIB) and especially in the phases of transmissions (from IIB to IIIA or from IIIA to IIIB). This can be the case in two ways.

In the first place, there can intervene as usual an action of the contents on the forms under construction, not because the forms may be derived from the contents, but because they favor their construction by imposing on the subject the necessity of going beyond the forms at his disposal. It is rather clearly the case in the evolution of proportions, when in level IIB we see intermediary solutions appearing between addition and multiplication. When there is a difference, $a > b$, the subject arrives at the idea that the adjunctions a' and b' must also respect the relationship $a' > b'$ without stopping at the equality $a' = b'$; the addition of several units then constitutes the beginning of the multiplicative process with addition of additions. It is therefore clear that this kind of feeling for proportionality, preceding its effective construction, will be especially reinforced in causal situations, even though we observe it in all areas in which this structure is involved. That the size of the effects are proportional to those of the causes constitutes almost an analytical truth once we admit that causality is something other than a regular succession and that it entails, strictly speaking, a production. In the case of distributivity (experiment of the elastic in R54), the substitution of the concept of homogeneous stretching for that of displacement requires the substitution of the idea of simple additive difference for that of coefficient. Now the idea of a coefficient no longer bears, as do the differences, on the static resultants alone, but on the transformation itself, from *a* to *na,* and thus leads to proportions and to distributivity.

But when it is a question of complex structures, such as those considered here, as opposed to the elementary compositions previously examined, a new factor appears, which, as a rule, was already in effect. When the structure, already formed in some situations, is applied to others, these "applications" constitute morphisms that enrich the area of the structure considered. When the application extends to "attributions," these morphisms then link the internal structures of the subject to those he discovers in reality, and he constructs for himself as many different morphisms as there will be distinct attributions. In this case, the causal or physical explanations of the subject will lead him to conceptual modifications, becoming all the richer and of a richness that increases in going from the geometric to the kinematic and dynamic, which will bring about changes of the structure into substructures with their own characteristics. In particular, if we refer to the vectoral operators described above, compositions will be produced between two or *n* operators; Cellérier forms the hypothesis of a "semigroup of operators" to the extent that this composition is associative.

It therefore seems clear, on the whole, that the applications of an operational structure constitute one of the factors of its development. In the physical domain, the prime mover of applications is the search for attribution itself.

13. The Composition of Two Heterogeneous Movements and Wave Motion

Before proceeding to problems of reactions, we still must ask ourselves of what the composition of two movements, nonhomogeneous in their sources and directions, consists, even though each is individually very simple. To this problem can be linked that of the complex coordination implied by the understanding of wave motion.

R56 supplies a particularly simple example of composition between two different movements. We throw a Ping-Pong ball horizontally, giving it a reverse spin so that after traveling a short distance straight ahead, it comes back. We find subjects from age 5 to 6 who succeed in imitating the action of the experimenter. Nevertheless, it is not until age 10 to 12 (stage III) that a complete explanation is obtained. In stage I the return of the ball is attributed to its lightness, speed, etc., to the table, to the air that pushes it, etc. In stage II it is due to the movements of the experimenter, but described in broad terms without the clear-cut distinction between the two movements in question as is the case when the subjects reach age 10 to 11.

R57 deals with an analogous problem, but one in which the two movements came from two distinct objects. A string unwinds as a result of the vertical descent of a spool around which it was wound, then, as the spool continues to turn when it reaches the end of its descent, the string rewinds and the spool goes back up. This is the toy called a Yo-Yo, with which most of our subjects were acquainted and which others began to operate before being given an explanation. Nevertheless, in level IA they consider all the effects as being due to the powers of the action itself or to those of the spool, which wants to go back up. Starting with level IB there is the beginning of objective analysis, but with some confusion about the actions of the spool and the string. In stage II the idea that predominates is that the momentum of the spool acquired in its descent allows it to go back up, this momentum being especially attributed to the action of the subject in IIA and to the spool itself in IIB. It is not until age 11 to 12 that the explanation is correct.

R58 deals with a more complex toy, the Bihip, in which two figures placed one in front of the other seem to walk as a result of a double balancing, both transversal (left–right) and longitudinal (legs), and to a slight traction (a light weight hung from the edge of the table and pulling the first figure) up to the time when the string is vertical and the traction ends. We can add a stick for balancing in order to facilitate the subjects' seeing the lateral movements of the dolls. In stage I everything is explained by traction, in

stage II the transversal balancing is, through a process of trial and
error, judged necessary, but without discovering the reason why.
Thus, when we stop the toy, the subject continues to push the
second figure from behind, instead of reactivating the lateral oscillations. In stage III, however, the coordination of the two movements is understood, as is the fact that the figures stop when they
reach the edge of the table.

The striking fact in R56 and 57 is that the subject does not
succeed in deriving sufficient information from his own action,
whether he imitates what he sees without understanding the reason
why, as in the case of the ball, or whether he overestimates the
role of the jerking movements he believes he must make instead of
limiting himself to holding the string, as in the case of the Yo-Yo.
The result is that the coordination of the two movements in question is achieved with as much difficulty as in the more complex
situation of R58. The reason is evidently that there are two heterogeneous movements to be coordinated. In this respect we could
think of a multiplication in the sense of a logical or qualitative
product, that is, to classify or seriate according to two criteria "at
the same time," as opposed to quantified or numerical multiplications. But if the multiplication of numbers is understood only
long after their addition, that of classes or of relationships in Cartesian products or matrices with a double or triple entry is no more
difficult than additive compositions. Therefore, in the case of movements as well known as the translation or rotation of a ball in R56
or the downward motion of a spool and the rewinding of a string in
R57, why is composition almost as difficult as in the case of the
tractions and balancing of R58? It is because in the case of two
classes, for example, x and y with their complements x' and y', the
four multiplicative associations xy, xy', $x'y$, and $x'y'$ are homogeneous in the sense that "$x \cdot$ non-y" is constructed in symmetry with
"non-$x \cdot y$." In the case of two distinct movements, the relationships
are more complex. In the case of the Ping-Pong ball, the rotation
combines with the direct translation, not like an inverse operation,
but like a kind of reciprocal which progressively compensates for it
before prevailing over it. We are therefore closer to a group of
quaternions with coordination of inverses and reciprocals than in
the case of the matrix of classes, where the passing from one

square to another stems from an elementary quaternity without this double reversibility. Likewise, in the case of the spool, its downward and upward movements do not have the same relationships with the string, since it is the downward movement that causes the string to unwind, whereas, in continuing to turn, the spool rewinds the string and is then pulled up by it. In the case of the Bibip the lateral balancing permits the horizontal traction, but when the latter stops, the balancing comes to an end.

In short, we are here in the presence of complex interactions without simple rules of composition and with a mixture of actions and of reactions the general form of which will be examined in the following paragraph. This complexity is found again in the case of wave motion, which has been studied under different forms:

R59 deals with the wave motion of a long spring, a Slinky, 3 to 4 m long, or of a rope the free end of which a child shakes, noting the spreading of the wave until it returns to the point of departure. In level IA he sees in the spring a kind of "ball" which travels and, in level IB, a segment of the spring or of the rope which travels as a result of a push, and not of an action of pulling. In stage II a ring cannot travel independently from others, but the subject continues to look for a simple translation in the spreading of the wave motion: that of a noise, of a light, of the air, etc. It is only at about age 10 to 11 (stage III) that we have a good analysis of the double movement of the wave, on the one hand, and of the upward and downward movements of the segments of the object, on the other hand.

R60 takes up these problems again in connection with wavelets produced by the fall of a drop of water in a little pool. In level IA it is the drop itself that moves by widening into waves. In level IB the drop moves up to the edges, but by combining with other drops. In stage II (age 7 to 10 and often beyond), the drop is limited to pushing the water around it in waves that are still thought of as translations. Again, it is only at age 11 to 12 (stage III) that the wave motion is understood.

R61 deals with the rising of water in an inclined helicoidal tube (Archimedes' screw). In addition to the movements of water, we must predict if and how a ring (watchband) placed around a ring or a paper glued on the glass will move. In level IA the liquid and the ring are supposed to turn and climb with the spiral in a general movement taking in both the container and the contents. Reading about the experiment in no way enlightens the subject. The same is true for level IB, but the ring begins to be seen sliding toward the bottom. In stage II the tube no longer moves forward, but the water rises without the subject's understanding that, in fact, the water is going down each time as it goes from one curve to the next. It is then pushed by air, by the momentum due to the rotation, etc. Finally, starting with age 11 (stage III), the movements are correctly analyzed.

We see to what degree these facts are consistent with all those that have already shown us the difficulties in the composition of directions. The problems of R56, R57, and R58 were solved only in the later stages because they included operations on operations and the question was one of coordinating heterogeneous movements. The spreading of the wave motion is an even more involved problem, because one of these movements is an alternance of rise and fall in one spot of parts or particles of the object, rings, or drops, whereas the other, the pulsations, consists of displacing not these particles themselves, as the subjects of stage I of R59 and R60 believe, but rather their movement of alternating rise and fall, only by transmitting it to the adjoining particles. Thus we have a transmission of movements, but of a very particular type since the movements are transmitted perpendicular to that of the transmission itself. It is therefore very normal that such a transmission to the second power is not understood before the stage of purely internal transmissions (see § 4), but it is remarkable that transmission is already understood at this stage, since it is a question of a kind of movement of movements.

In fact, the problem is solved, as in the case of the pairs of heterogeneous movements examined at the beginning of this section, by a system of quarternions whose observable elements are the following: for the parts of the object it is their rise (a)↑ and their fall (b)↓, and for the sinusoids of the pulsations it is their rise (c)↗ and their fall (d)↘. We find again these four components in the helicoidal tube of R60, but with the additional condition of coordinating the two internal and external systems of reference. Therein, therefore, is a structure that we shall now find again in its most general form in regard to action and reaction.

14. Action and Reaction and Reciprocities

The understanding of causal relationships necessarily comprises a certain reciprocity between the actions of the active and the passive objects. The central idea is that of transmission conceived as both the source of production, at least a kinematic modification of the passive object, and of relative conservation, since some movement, etc., is transmitted without disappearing. Moreover, if there is transmission, what the passive object B gains is lost for the active mobile A which, in the case of equality of form and of quantity of matter between them, does not yet imply any reciprocity except for those aspects of equivalence between gains and losses. On the other hand, as soon as there is inequality there is a problem. If B is heavier than A, even at level IB (age 5 to 6) half of the subjects admit that the weight of B decreases the action of A, although, for others, the weight of B reinforces that of A and B will go farther than when the weights are equal. There is, therefore, somewhat precociously, the intervention of a concept of resistance in the form of a simple braking, and this concept gains more and more ground in the course of stage II. But we are still far from the complete reciprocity expressed by Newton's third law. Indeed, in the concept of reaction there intervene two new properties which are very distinct from those of simple resistance as the source of braking: the equality in intensity of the action and reaction and the opposition of directions, therefore with a vectoral aspect, not explicit in the seventeenth century (Descartes' laws of impact, in particular, are almost all partially erroneous for lack of this consideration),[1] but implicitly very much present in this third law. Having stated this, it is now necessary to examine the formation of this structure of action and reaction, to verify its relationships with vectoral compositions, and to determine what operations constitute its attribution, which will lead us to analyze other forms of reciprocities.

R62 deals with actions and reactions in cases of simple thrusts. The adult and the child each push a similar coin into both sides of

[1] Not to mention the absence of a clear distinction between kinetic energy and quantity of movement.

a lump of modeling clay; the question concerns simply the depth of the two penetrations. In level IA the subject goes no further than evaluating the forces of thrusts, without considering resistances nor even the relationships between the penetration and the forces indicated. "You push very hard and me not so hard," says Flo at 4;0; therefore, the penetrations will be "both the same thing." At level IB (component functions), the penetration is the function of the thrusting force except for a reference to the action of "holding back" when the question carries the suggestion of it. In level IIA there appear thrusts and resistances, which go hand in hand with the first signs of operational reversibility as if they were sequential, not simultaneous, or with series of incorrect inequalities. These are the simultaneous reciprocities that the subjects of level IIB struggle to grasp but often with the idea, peculiar to mediate transmissions —which are semi-internal and semi-external in stage II—that the thrusts and resistances make the lump move and that thus one partner pushing against the other aids the penetration in the opposite direction. Finally, in stage III, there is understanding of the equality of the penetrations because "when you were pushing I was holding back and when I was pushing you were holding back" simultaneously and "that makes the same force" because to a stronger thrust by the adult corresponds a stronger resistance by the child and to a weaker thrust there is a corresponding weaker reaction. Likewise, when the child pushes the adult, both being on roller skates, the subjects of stage III, although they do not consider speeds, etc., anticipate and understand their recoil: "It's the opposite effect," "it is the thrust and the recoil," "it's like the principle of cannons," etc., and, with an arrow gun, "the gun recoils when the bullet leaves," etc.

R63 deals with the movement of an inflated balloon in the direction opposite that from which the air escapes when it is being deflated. In level IA there is no anticipation of directions nor understanding of a causal link between the motion of the balloon and the escape of the air. In level IB this link is confirmed, but the air current on escaping remains without a stable direction and manages to draw the balloon in the desired directions. In level IIA the air is divided: one half escapes backwards and the other half pushes forward from inside the balloon, which is partially true, but for very different reasons. In level IIB the air escapes and bounces either against the walls of the room or against the surrounding air, and it is the return thus produced that propels the balloon forward. In level IIIA this hypothesis of rebounding is still often raised, but linked with the ideas of pressure and recompression which already imply the reaction. Finally, in level IIIB, the reaction is understood as a necessary consequence of the air's escaping without there being any longer the necessity of a rebound.

R64 studied the rebound itself in the case of a rubber ball that is dropped. In stage I the ball bounces up both because we make it bounce up and because it has the power to, it is "made for it," "it is round on all sides." In the course of stage II, we find three types of responses: (a) It bounces up because it is heavy, which favors its fall, "it gets its impetus from the ground and then it bounces back"; (b) it bounces up because it is light, which favors its going up; (c) it is "flexible," elastic, etc., which is still only a tautology without explanation. Indeed, when we rub the ball with talcum powder, which makes its flattening out on the table visible, the subjects of stage II clearly foresee that the flattening out will be all the greater when the ball falls from a greater height, but they consider it as hindering the bouncing up and not the opposite. It is only in stage III that the rebound is explained by a reaction understood as a tendency of the ball to resume its shape, this tendency being all the stronger the greater the deformation by flattening.

All the facts combine, therefore, to show that the notion of a reaction in the opposite direction of the action, as opposed to a resistance conceived as a simple braking, is not developed until stage III (about age 11 to 12), at a level when the forces are composed on a vectorial mode. This synchronism is again reinforced by an examination of the reactions within liquids.

A former study on hydraulic pressure, with B. Inhelder, had already established this synchronism. The apparatus consisted of a U tube in which a piston on the right could be loaded with weights; the level of the water on the left depended not only on these weights but also on the density of the liquid—whether it was pure water, alcohol, or diluted glycerine. It is again only in stage III that the liquid is understood as exerting a reaction in the direction opposite that of the weights of the piston; until then, the only direction considered is that of the thrust, as though the weight of the liquid acted in the same direction as that of the piston.

R65 took up the problem again in a simpler form. Into two vertical tubes, 50 × 10 cm, filled with water or alcohol, we put little barrels of the same weight and volume, then of different weights with equal volumes, different volumes with equal weights, and finally, different volumes and weights but with compensation. The questions bore on the speeds of the fall, which were rather slow to facilitate easy comparison. As far as the weight is concerned, the subjects of stage I attribute no role to it or think that the lightness of the barrel favors its descent to the same degree as its heaviness. In stage II the fall is due to absolute weight, whereas in stage III it is coordinated with the volume. As for the volume, it is at first neglected in favor of the weight or identified by the weight as if heaviness were a function of size. When there is a contradiction with the facts, the contradiction is removed by compromises according to which, for example, the little barrel "has something big inside it" (Sti at 6;8). In the course of stage II the volume is progressively disassociated and considered as the cause of the slowing down, but by simple braking: "It puts the brakes on," "the size holds it back," etc. Finally, in stage III, and particularly in comparisons between alcohol and water, the volume releases the "pressure" of the water going in the opposite direction of the descent of the barrel: "The pressure goes up" (Joy 12;10), etc.

This understanding of the different fields of a reaction going in the direction opposite to that of the action and being of equal intensity, therefore presupposes vectoral directions; this is the primary reason why it is manifested only in stage III. But this is not the only reason. The formation of this reaction immediately following an action, and especially the fact that these two forces oppose each other without canceling, are still to be understood. Indeed, an opposition of directions without cancellation constitutes an operational connection different from the inversion, which is a negation, that is, a cancellation, and it corresponds to a reciprocity. If the composition of an operation with its inverse amounts to its cancellation $(+A - A = 0)$, the product of two reciprocals, here two equivalent or opposing forces, although acting on different points, consists of a compensation, and therefore of a cancellation, of the differences and not of the terms themselves. If, starting with age 7 to 8, reciprocity intervenes in the operation of relationships at the same time as inversion for the operations of classes, the new condition that the composition of actions and reactions must satisfy is the simultaneous utilization of inversions and reciprocities and their composition from each other, therefore, the construction of a system of two reversibilities, since the action as well as the reaction can give rise to increases $(+)$ or decreases $(-)$, but, in addition, every variation of the first entails a reciprocity of the second. Therefore, there intervenes here a structure isomorphic to that which, in the field of interpropositional operations of the subject, constitutes a group INRC; this composition is possible only in stage III, where intervenes the "totality of parts," which is both combinatory and the source of propositional operations, and therefore of group INRC.

But in the case of causal actions and reactions, this operational structure is naturally "attributed" to objects, even with a matrix of nine squares according to the values $+$, $=$, and $-$ for each of these two dimensions. This "attribution" is, moreover, so evident that the logician Parson, in his criticism of our work with B. Inhelder, in which the application of this structure to the induction of physical laws is already developed, believed that we were thus describing the physical facts themselves, without realizing that we were concerned with the operations of the subject. Actually, the subject goes no further in his search for laws than the application of his own operations, while with the causal explanation the attribution becomes necessary to "understand" the process at work.

The role of reciprocity asserts itself not only in these three general systems of actions and reactions, it also occurs in cases of circular causality or feedback.

Thus, R66 deals with an example of positive feedback in which a vertical bar, acting as a balancing bar, allows, by dipping, the passage of one marble after another in zigzags along a slope. In the process of descending, each marble hits the bottom of the balance bar, which in the meantime has resumed its vertical position, making it dip and opening the way for a new marble at the top of the apparatus. Although no explicit causality intervenes in level IA, starting with level IB the children succeed in understanding the connection between the impact of the marble against the bottom of the bar and the opening resulting from it at the top that "lets the next marble go through." But the subject sees in it a one-way process, and does not wonder why the balance bar resumes its vertical position between two marbles. In the course of stage II, progress is noticed only in sensing the necessity of the action of the marble at the bottom of the course, which "necessarily" displaces the top of the bar with a retroactive effect on the next marble. In level IIB, however, some subjects observe that the balance bar "moves" without stopping, and wonder "why it turns." But it is not until stage III that the balancing is noted and that the return of the bar, "which returns to its position," is understood as constituting the necessary condition for the closure of the circuit. It is therefore only at this level that reciprocity is understood in a situation of semicircular causality in which, however, everything is visible.

A little more complicated course is analyzed in R67. A box provided with two openings, *A* and *B*, is presented to the child, and we place near *A*, on the outside, a smoke-producing substance. The subject notices that, when it is by itself, its smoke rises like any other. Under opening *B* we light a candle in the box. In this case the warm air passes through *B*, creating a vacuum in the box, and the smoke on the outside enters *A* and rejoins the air heated by the candle, so that it goes out through *B* following a circuit that is incomplete but sufficient to pose a problem. In stage I the phenomenon is explained only by the powers and the intentions of the smoke. In level IIA the subjects look for two independent explanations for the processes in *A* and *B*. In level IIB there is a search for unity, which is not entirely successful, and the subject ends up by finding compromises such as "the blue of the flame attracts the smoke, the yellow pushes it away." Finally, at about age 11 to 12 (stage III), the whole process is understood, including the attraction of the air produced by the hot air that rises in *B*.

The facts in R66 are interesting in that everything in the elements of the circuit is easily explained, and the movements of a balance bar are understood precociously, but, in spite of this, the circuit as such becomes clear only later on. However, the retroactive character of the action of one marble on the next is grasped starting with level IB, even though the next marble is set in motion at the top of the apparatus well after the first, while the first has stopped rolling and is leaving the circuit at the bottom of the descent just when it is acting on the second. But this action through the intermediary of the bar is understood as if it were a question of pulling a mobile 50 cm by means of a long string. On the other hand, the return of the balance bar to its vertical position, even though perfectly understandable, plays a role in the circuit comparable to that of a reaction—and that is what creates the problem. If we call x the downward slope of the balance bar, x' the upward slope, and y or y' the passage of a marble either downward (y' by dipping the balance bar) or upward (y as a result of this slope), we have in effect the four following functions:

$$(a) \quad x' = f(y'); \quad (b) \quad y = f(x); \quad (c) \quad \bar{y} = f(\bar{x});$$
$$\text{and} \quad (d) \bar{x}' = f(\bar{y}')$$

Function (d) intervenes when the first marble goes down before pushing the bar (therefore, before going through).

If functions (a) and (b) are already discovered in stage II and even partially in level IB, they are not sufficient to ensure the closure of the circuit, even though they constitute a kind of reciprocity through permutation of terms. To close the circuit, we need a coordination of reciprocities with inversions, and therefore the adjunction of functions (d) and (c), which imply the return of the bar to the vertical position, not made explicit spontaneously until stage III. Indeed, the composition of the four functions in question constitutes a group of quaternity. If (b) is the R of (a), then (c) is the NR and therefore the correlate C of A, and (d), which is N of (a), is therefore, for this reason, its RC. Thus we find again the same structure as in the process of action and reaction, and it is therefore not by chance that we must wait until stage III for the total process to be made explicit, even though each of its elements is comprehensible by itself.

The circuit in R67 is more complex, since the subject sees neither the heat rising in B nor the resulting vacuum. Therefore, he does not see the action of the combustion in B on the smoke in A, which draws up the air. Moreover and above all, the problem is to invert the apparent order of succession, since the source of the circuit is in B and not in A as it would first appear. Nevertheless, the four processes of the rising of the air in B, its action on A, the downward movement of smoke in A, and its rising in B are coordinated at the same level, age 11, as those of R66.

15. The Principles of Sufficient Reason
and Inertia

Up to now we have seen the main outlines of operational composition attributed to objects. These are transitivity (§§ 4–5),
reversibility (§ 6), additivity (§§ 7–8), multiplicativity (§§ 9–12),
and reciprocity (§ 14). However, a regulating principle appears
in the compositions depending on the operations of the subject,
the explicit applications of which are slow in coming and concern
especially the deductions reached, but the implicit meaning of
which is more precocious and becomes general, starting with
stage III, from hypothetico-deductive reasonings, that is, the principle of sufficient reason. It can present itself in four forms,
whether we speak only of "reason" (*nil est sine ratione,* said
Leibniz) or insist on its "sufficient" quality, and whether we express it in its positive or negative aspects. The first of these forms
(IA), therefore, amounts to saying that every state and every
change has a certain number of necessary conditions, and, in the
negative form (IB), that if one of these conditions is not met, the
effect is not produced: *Sublate causa, tollitur effectus.* The third
and fourth forms are more interesting. In order to produce the
state or the change, a certain number of conditions brought together are sufficient (IIA). We then have two negative consequences according to whether we place ourselves inside or outside
the boundaries of this group of conditions. In the first place, if
these conditions are not all met, the effect is not produced that
leads us back to IB but, in the second place (IIB), there is no
reason for others to intervene, in addition to those that are
sufficient.

Thus stated, it is evident that this or these principles of sufficient reason are only regulatory, like formal principles of logic.
That is why the principle of contradiction forbids us to contradict
ourselves, but it does not tell us what is contradictory and what
is not. We therefore know only that a is incompatible with $\bar{a}$ (or
$a|\bar{a}$), but this does not tell us whether b implies $\bar{a}$ or whether it is
compatible with a; the question must be settled by the inferences
drawn from detailed definitions. The same holds true for the prin-

ciples of sufficient reason. Aristotle, admitting that every movement depends on an "external motor," concluded that when separated from that motor, a mobile no longer has any reason to keep its movement even in a straight line, the "internal motor" not being "sufficient." On the contrary, by making inertial movement a stable state, Galileo and Descartes concluded that, except for external resistances, there is no reason for such a movement to end.

Nevertheless, despite the fact that their character is only regulatory, these principles of sufficient reason are not by nature exclusively methodological, but give rise to certain "attributions" to the objects themselves, particularly in the IIB form from which Fermat and Maupertuis derived their principles of least action, founded, by one, on the choice of the best course, etc., and, by the other, on a kind of natural economy of the quantities of action. Such principles interest us for two reasons. In the first place, they apply to operational as well as causal structures. It is thus that an axiomatic reasoning can be used to establish the necessary and sufficient conditions of a system—for example, the bivalent logic of propositions—and, in this case, the axioms, while remaining distinct, must be reduced to the minimum without any redundancy, from which we get the reduction of five axioms to four initially postulated by Whitehead and Russell, one of which proved to be useless. In the second place, the same principles can be "attributed" to the objects themselves and then can take on a causal meaning, because, as Leibniz said, "cause in things corresponds to reason in truths" (*Nouveaux essais,* IV, Chap. XVII, § 3).

In this respect the IIB form of the principle can give rise to two kinds of attributions. First, there are the problems relative to the paths traveled or to the temporal processes, like Fermat's optical path, problems that stem from what we call today the "principles of *extremum.*" In general, it is a question of minimal actions, the shortest path among all the neighboring paths, but at times maximal, particularly in the case of increasing probability. Sometimes the two are even combined, as when the *minimum* of potential energy, toward which a mobile tends at the bottom of a slope, corresponds to an increase in kinetic energy during the fall. Second, we can say, in general, that in stationary symmetrical states, like those we are going to discuss, there is no reason for a change to occur, while the asymmetries constitute reasons for transformations. Finally, if we have tried in vain, from Euler to Maxwell, to "explain" the principle of inertia through sufficient reason, since we have seen above that reason explains nothing as long as we do not define in advance precisely what are the necessary and sufficient conditions at work in the process to be interpreted, it seems clear that, once the straight line is recognized as the shortest path and the uniform and rectilinear movement as a state, and not as a temporary change, the IIB form of the principle requires its conservation.

R68 and 69 furnish us with examples of *extremum*. In the course of R68, we asked the subject to predict and explain the placement of 1 to 19 beads which we put one by one in a watch crystal or all at once but in no order, and which, when shaken, fall immediately into a regular pattern in straight rows. In stage I, the first bead will go to the middle and the others anywhere, or else in the middle, conceived as a median, each acting on its own. In stage II there are interactions, and the final form is explained as being the most stable, that is, the one that excludes any new displacement. Finally, in stage III, all the beads go toward the lowest point, resulting in the *minimum* distance in relation to the center, the *minimum* surface, and the *maximum* density, the straight lines being due to the fact that "they line up against each other; if there are no spaces they can only be in straight lines."

R69 uses a circular frame placed in a dish containing soapy water. On the layer of soap that forms inside the frame we place a knotted thread. When we prick the layer inside the thread, the thread immediately takes the form of a perfect circle. After an explanation, we ask the subjects to predict what will happen inside a square frame. In the course of stage I they attribute the circle to the powers of the experimenter or of the soap, etc., and do not assume that, by repeating the experiment, the circle will necessarily be reproduced. In stage II the circle is due to the hole that was made in the layer of soap or to the interior or exterior thrust acting in a homogeneous fashion "on all sides," which brings us close to sufficient reason. In stage III there is added the idea of maximization: "It goes out in all directions and it makes it round . . . because that is where there is the most room," and some add that, with another form, "it takes more string."

Briefly, the shape of the beads in the watch crystal or of the thread in the layer of soap are due to the equalization of effects none of which has any reason to be more important than the others. Of course, here it is a question of forms of equilibrium and not of the shortest path. However, on the one hand, the principle of virtual speeds is not far from that of sufficient reason, because we can maintain that, if two virtual operations compensate each other, it is because there is no reason, such as inequalities or asymmetries, for one to win over the other. On the other hand, we see that with the subjects of stage III in these two studies, the absence of inequalities between the effects entails, in addition, ideas of *extremum*. The equality of thrusts ends in the elimination of all lost space, resulting in a surface that is minimal for a given whole of beads that are close together but that is maximal in the case of the stretched thread surrounding the layer of soap.

Let us note again how much these explanations are both rational and mechanistic, despite the finalism that Max Planck wanted to attribute to the concept of least action, and we find them among the subjects, age 10 to 12, for whom physics, a few years before, was permeated with an Aristotelian common sense.

On the other hand, the problem of inertia is much more complex because, in order to arrive at the understanding that there is no reason for an acquired movement to change speed or direction in the absence of any intervention by an outside force, it is necessary, on one hand, to admit that any nonrectilinear movement changes direction even if it is circular, and, on the other hand, to resist the sum total of daily facts that appear to be contradictory. Thus, previously, with B. Inhelder, we found only a few subjects, age 13 to 15, who maintained that, if the stopping a of a mobile is due to friction, to the resistance of the air, etc., for instance, $a \supset b \vee c \vee d \vee \ldots$, then the elimination of these causes entails the conservation of movement or $\overline{b \cdot c \cdot d \cdots} \supset \bar{a}$. On the other hand, it is interesting to study the progress of the concept of inertia as temporary conservations between stages I to IIIB.

R70 deals with the problems of knowing (1) on which side a child will fall when standing on a rug if we pull it in a given direction, (2) the same for a doll standing on a piece of cardboard,

(3) where one must place a person in a carriage so that he does not fall when the carriage starts, (4) what will happen to a marble at the rear of a carriage when the carriage starts and then when it stops, and (5) the same situation if the marble is placed in the middle. At stage I, problems 1 and 2 are not solved any better than the others. At stage II, most of the subjects solve problems 1 and 2, and many even solve problem 3, but problems 4 and 5 give rise to a false and rather systematic prediction. The marble will start at the same time and in the same direction as the carriage by an immediate transmission of its movement and without the subject's suspecting that the marble would thus have a speed double that of the carriage. Finally, in stage III, the subjects admit that when they start, the marbles go in the opposite direction, and even stay in place relative to the exterior references, and that, when they stop, they take on by transmission the movement of the carriage and go forward.

R6, already cited (§ 4), uses as an apparatus the rotation of a horizontal angle-iron that we strike near one of its extremities. On the side hit, the marble placed on the angle-iron is projected forward, while on the other side, a second marble falls vertically, staying immobile through inertia, on a support slipping from under it. Considering here only the second marble, we note that in stage I the subject makes no distinction between the two situations, except that the marble falls with less force when it is situated farther from the impact. In level IIA the marble not propelled is still supposed to start out just the same in the direction of rotation, although the subject clearly notes the differences of intensity still attributed to the distance from the point of impact. Level IIB is characterized by intermediary reactions, the subject sometimes understanding that the second marble is not propelled, but distorting this intuition through pseudodynamic considerations (vibrations, etc.). In level IIIA the subject succeeds, through trial and error, in understanding the passive character of the fall of this marble, but does not yet grasp the role of the vertical edge of the angle-iron nor especially of its absence in the direction in which the nonpropelled marble falls. Finally, the subject in level IIIB has the correct solution, beginning with the anticipations, the role of the edge being understood.

R71, concerning centrifugal force, furnishes indications on the tangential direction of the start of mobiles on a rotating disc. In stage I the trajectories are first inconsequential, then have a tendency to go in a circle on the disc itself with no anticipation of falls, which is still frequent at age 7 and beyond. In stage II the fall is anticipated but the initial direction is predicted as being perpendicular to the edge of the disc (still by a fourth or a third of the subjects, age 9 to 10, and sometimes beyond that age), behind it, or a little in front of it. Finally, in stage III, the initial direction is tangential. The situations dealing with a roller coaster rail when a marble is forced to start at the point of a sharp curve or on a horizontal course, but with a hairpin turn, give the same results.

These various facts together show that it takes a long time to understand the inertial processes, and one can easily see why. Admitting that a marble moves back in relation to a support in motion and stays in place in relation to external references is both to resist the suggestions of transmissions and to coordinate two systems of reference. On the other hand, the conservation of a rectilinear and uniform movement, especially when it manifests itself after the support stops, as in R70, is not a conservation like any other, since it deals with the movement as a state and not with static properties. It presupposes, therefore, something other than a play of additive identities, neither taking away nor adding anything, of reversibilities or compensations. It implies, as our former subjects cited above said, an analysis of the causes of the stopping and the deductive conclusion that, in their absence, there is no longer a reason for the movement to stop. In other words, the inertial conservation of the movement is undoubtedly the most inferential of the causal connections as well as the most necessary among the operational structures attributed to the object because, like the principle of sufficient reason of which it is an expression, it constitutes a preliminary condition of both the coherence of reality and the intelligibility of the phenomena.

16. *"Weight" and Its Compositions with Spatial Dimensions*

The development of the concept of "weight" is perhaps the most complex and the most difficult to analyze in detail, because the term covers two different concepts in physics that are not recognized either by the child or by adult common sense: that of mass or quantity of matter and that of the weight itself, which is the result on the mass of the force of gravity directed toward the center of the earth. But the mass itself plays a dynamic active role in the composition of force, $f = ma,$ therefore $m = f/a$ and a role of double resistance when it starts and when it stops. As for weight, it is at all levels considered a force or, more precisely, a coefficient of action, although not at first directed downwards. Since weight is not differentiated from mass, we can understand the complexities of the problems it raises for the subject and also for the observer trying to understand what the subject is trying to say.

Generally speaking and conserving the multivocal term "weight" in order to remain faithful to the children's vocabulary, we observe a succession of phases going from undifferentiation to differentiations between what we shall call weight-quantity, or property of a body, and weight-action, or manifestation of varied dynamic effects. As for weight-action, its coordination with weight-quantity can scarcely take place before the child realizes that weight is composed of spatial dimensions. There is the spatial dimension of volume when it comes to density and its assumed corpuscular models, or when it comes to flotation. There is the dimension of surface when it comes to pressure and of lengths or distances when it comes to time or performance. Indeed, it is only with such compositions that the dynamics of weight-action begins to be structured and to be integrated with weight-quantities, while still in level IIB, which is that of the conservation of weight-quantity when the shape of the object changes, the subject is satisfied with compromises according to which the weight remains invariant but "gives" or "weighs," etc., variably according to actions or even different positions. But it is not until stage III that the composition of weights with spatial dimensions becomes possible, because the subjects presuppose the construction of relationships as well as vectoral operations (themselves combining forces and directions, therefore spatial relations) as well as proportions, distributivity, etc.—in short, a group of operations on operations.

R72 deals with the outflow of water in three pipes, downward, horizontal, and upward from a pool, as well as with the movements of a marble on an incline. Weight is taken into account in the case of the marble only in level IIA; we recall that the same is true for the ruler falling from the edge of the table in R15, as we saw in § 6. As for the water, weight does not appear until level IIB because until then it is considered light. In stage I water goes down because it is "fine," etc., and the marble goes down because it rolls. In level IIA there is added the idea that the incline, until then considered simply as the only open path, becomes the source of the impetus.

R16, which was discussed in § 6, deals with the fall of objects lined up on the edge of the table and with their equilibrium when they are placed on a cylindrical support, with or without additional weights attached by suction cups. In stage I the equilibrium is anticipated without reference to weight, except when the suction cups intervene, but in this case, without understanding the equilibrium. A 6-year-old subject, for example, correctly shows the symmetrical distribution of the weights of the parts of the circle when he is asked about them, but he does not succeed in placing the suction cups so as to maintain equilibrium. In level IIA, weight is always brought up, and in level IIB, several partitions are possible for the same object, which leads, in stage III, to the understanding of the center of gravity, the point where partitions intersect. Another analogous study (R73), with forks stuck in a cork at different heights and at different angles, has shown the role of symmetries in a precocious anticipation, starting with stage I but without quantification at that point. The weight of the forks is located in their free ends, and the fall is foreseen along the line of extension of their angles. This anticipation still exists in level IIA, but the weight of the object is located at its point of insertion, where it "pulls," and there is detailed quantification. In level IIB the falls are anticipated as vertical, and in stage III the subject finds compensations between the positions and the weights.

R48 studied the composition of the weights on a tray placed on top of a rod, which sinks more or less deeply into synthetic moss according to the load. In level IA there are no relationships between the weights and the penetrations. In level IIB the relationship is found, but it is ordinal and without additivity, the weight of two (or n) plugs depending on how they are placed. In stage IIA there is additivity and conservation of a weight independent of its position, while in IIB, the action of the weight varies with its position, that is, weights piled up or juxtaposed, etc. In stage III additivity reappears, based on the equality of volumes.

R47, in which weights were hung in opposite directions, gave analogous results, with the same contrast between levels IIA and IIB but the additivity in stage III justified by the equality of the forces.

R20, already cited, also deals with the unchanging equilibrium of two equal weights hung at various heights from the same string held by a pulley. In level IA the weight does not intervene or stays little quantified. In IB the weight raised is heavier and tends to go down. In level IIA the weights become constant, but they have a tendency to come together at the same height. In IIB their action varies with the height, and the lowest will go down even further. In stage III the situation is understood. In R74 a big plug placed flat on a slight incline is pulled up by a weight hung vertically at the end of the track. In stage I there are no regular relationships between the weights, nor is there conservation as seen in R18, which deals with suspensions. In stage I the value of the counterweight is not yet taken into account, as long as it is in a holding position. When the plug and the weight are compared with one another in a vertical suspension, the subject does not see any contradiction in maintaining that in this case the weight is lighter than the plug, but that it is heavier when it pulls the plug in the first situation. In stage II the weight stays the same, and, if the plug, which is at first judged lighter than the weight pulling it, is then noted to be heavier, its movement is attributed to how easily it slides, etc. In stage III the situation is understood in terms of the direction of forces. Let us note that in R19, with the carriage on an incline, we asked if it required more force to pull it or push it, on an incline or horizontally, and according to the placement of the loads in front of, behind, or in the middle of the carriage. It is not until stage III that there is equivalence, and then it is still only in a horizontal position.

R75 confirmed and analyzed the fact that a pebble dropped in water makes the water rise because of its weight and not its volume, the latter not becoming a decisive factor until stage III. In level IA the water level will not change. In IB it will go up or down due to the movement of the pebble because, if the pebble is first placed in the glass, the water will have the same level as though it were not there. In level IIA the weight makes the water rise even if the solid is placed in advance; the lower the solid goes, the higher the water rises. A pierced ball also makes the water rise because, when it is filled, it becomes heavy and acts on the rest of the water. In level IIB the reactions are intermediate because of a connection between the weight and the "bigness," but the problem of the pierced ball is not always solved as it is in stage III, where the role of the volume is understood. Let us recall that in R39 the horizontality of the water is not explained before level IIB (9;6 to 11;00) by its weight and by its role in the tendency of the water to go down, the water being up to that point judged to be light.

The floating of solids has been studied previously with B. Inhelder.[1] It was taken up again in R21 with liquids of different densities: Three glasses contain water and alcohol mixed according to densities $d_1 > D$, $d_2 = D$, and $d_3 < D$ in connection with the density D of oil that a child pours with the same eyedropper. Up to and including level IIA, the water is supposed to stay the same in the three glasses, whereas the oil is considered, even though it comes from the same receptacle, as if it were different in quantity from one glass to another. In level IIB it is the opposite, but without spontaneous allusions to the relative weight. Weight intervenes only in stage III, with the consideration of volume, equal volumes having different weights.

R76 deals with the floating of sheets of composition board of different sizes on which are attached weights that are also variable. In level IA the weight but not the size is mentioned, and, with the polyvalence customary at this level, it can just as easily make the board float as make it sink. In level IB the size of the sheets is considered, but is finally assimilated with the weight. In level IIA the weight tends to sink it, and the composition board to hold it back in terms of its size but, since the board comprises a heavier weight, the subject senses a contradiction without resolving it. In level IIB the resistance of the water is added, in the substage where it becomes heavy (as seen in R72). In stage III the explanation is found by putting into relationships the surfaces (IIIA) and then the combined volumes and the weights of the board compared to the same volume of water (IIIB).

R77 deals with the weight of objects according to their positions, vertical or horizontal, etc., with its location in the object and with the transmission of its action when they are piled up. In stage I the multiple forms of the weight, that is, pulling, carrying, weighing on, etc., are neither coordinated nor even characterized in a regular way. In level IIA we observe a differentiation between the weight-quantity and the weight-actions, but without coordination. In the

[1] See B. Inhelder and J. Piaget, *De la logique de l'enfant à la logique de l'adolescent* (P.U.F.).

questions of transitivity, the higher object does not exert weight on the table through the others, but each carries more weight than the preceding one. In level IIB the coordination begins, and transitivity or transmission no longer poses a problem. In stage III the solidarity of the parts of the objects, corpuscular models, is added.

R78 deals with the pressure exerted by the penetration of plugs according to their surfaces and their weight, and with the transmission of compression when a plug is placed on empty plastic cubes of negligible weight. In level IA this transmission is denied, in level IB there is wavering, but in level IIA it is accepted without further hesitation and with cumulative effects. In level IIB the cubes transmit more or less pressure because they restrain the action (transmission × resistance), and in stage III there is transmission with conservation of the effect. As for the pressure itself, in stage I weight alone intervenes, and in stage IIA resistances without mention of surfaces are added. The role of the surfaces is recognized after having been noted in level IIB and correctly anticipated in stage III.

The role of pressure has been analyzed in R79 in connection with a cylindrical tube provided with three openings at different heights from which escape jets of water, the lengths of which vary with the pressure of the liquid. In stage I these lengths are predicted in terms of the height at which the holes are placed, and even in level IIA the water is supposed to rise as well as go down to join the openings from which it spurts out. After noting the lengths of the jets, it only goes down. From age 9 to 10 (IIB), and especially in stage III, the prediction is good but the pressure is evaluated in terms of the volume and not of the surface. As far as air is concerned, when this inverse relationship with the volume is correct, we shall see that the pressure in terms of the diminishing volume is understood in stage III (R94, etc.; see § 20). On the other hand, in the case of connected vessels of unequal diameters, the concept of atmospheric pressure is not understood, but yet, coming closer to a weight relative to the surface, the subjects of stage III at times bring up the idea of an equilibrium of "powers," therefore, in the sense of pressures or of weights distinct from those measured on the scale (R80).

Finally, R81 used a wheelbarrow with long handles grasped at different distances from the weight to be lifted. In stage I the length of the handles facilitates the action without transmission of the effects of the weight. This weight being situated at the other end does not act along the length of the handles. In stage II the weight acts, but less so, or is "less felt," whereas in stage III the composition of the weight with the length gives rise to intuitions of when and especially how it works, as we shall see.

From these multiple facts it is thus possible to conclude that there are five or even six levels characterized, as already indicated, by a passage from undifferentiation between weight-quantity and weight-action to their differentiation and their final coordination. Stage I is that of undifferentiation, in which the weight, without even always using this word, is a function of "bigness," but insofar as both the quantity of matter and the seat of the various powers are concerned. In level IA this "bigness" is still quantified only in ordinal numbers, so that the equilibrium in situations of balance is not generally predicted except for precocious symmetries, symmetries inspired by the case of the body itself and mentioned in § 6 (the ruler going beyond the edge of the table, etc.). In level IB some compensations ensuring equilibrium are partially understood, but without conservation of weight according to their position whether piled up, juxtaposed, hung from a short or long string, etc., and consequently, without additivity being possible. Stage II is that of a differentiation between weight-quantity and weight-action, the progress of each being noted but limited in use by the lack of coordination between them. In level IIA weight-quantity acquires an elementary sort of conservation, that of the weight of the object when only its position is changed. That conservation is not yet understood when the shape of the object is modified, resulting in a possible additivity, this conservation and this additivity therefore marking a beginning of operational composition as found in § 6. From the point of view of weight-action, progress is then noted in situations of equilibrium, but when it comes to directions followed by the weight considered as force, we observe a curious and rather systematic gap. The weight does not always go down vertically and, in some cases, does not even have a tendency to go down. R73, for example, shows that at this substage, if we let go a ruler held in an inclined position, it still goes down in the direction of its own extension, and not vertically. Likewise, R72 and 39 show that the downward flow of water is not attributed to its weight, because water is thought to be light. The role of the incline opened at the lower end is still that of a free space, as opposed to external obstacles preventing the rise, and the level of the water is neither recognized as being horizontal nor explained by the weight. The cart on an inclined plane in R19 requires more force to hold it in place because of its tendency to go down than it requires to raise it, because when it rises this tendency disappears.

In substage IIB, on the other hand, two noteworthy modifications are observed in connection with weight-quantity and weight-action. The first becomes capable of conservation even when the shape of the object changes, for example, when a clay ball is rolled like a sausage or cut up in pieces. The second is henceforth conceived as moving downward and vertically. The progress in both these instances is important, in the first by generalizing the connection of weight with the quantity of matter, and in the second by ensuring the connection of weight-action with the systems of natural coordinates, that is, verticality of the downward movement and horizontality of the water resulting from it; this progress is made in the same substage, IIB. But what is still lacking is the composition of these two ideas of weight-quantity and weight-action, henceforth better differentiated in the two directions of mass and of dynamism in general. This lack of sufficient coordination explains in particular the fact that the synthesis of the idea of force is not yet possible at this level, even though the connection of the weight with the geometric systems of reference marks a first step in the direction of its spatialization. Indeed, from the fact that the weight tends to go down vertically, the subjects of level IIB will conclude, for example, that it acts and "weighs" more toward the bottom than the top or that it is unequally distributed in the object, etc., this apparent regression to nonadditivity being due to the progress of dynamism and also to the lack of coordination with weight-quantity.

In order for that coordination to take place, we must have a condition in addition to a simple determination of directions. It is necessary to link weight, as a quantifiable property of objects, to their spatial dimensions in general. The most important of these connections is the one of weight and volume, resulting in the idea of density and the solution of the problems of floating. Concerning the latter we can even distinguish two levels, one of them IIIA, in which weight becomes relative to surfaces, the other IIIB, in which it is ascribed to volume as such. In this last case we clearly understand the coordination between weight-quantity and weight-action since, by comparing the weight of the bodies, taking their volume into consideration, to the weight of equal volumes of water, the subject simultaneously calls upon weight-quantities and on an interaction dependent on them. The concept of density [2] can be developed only in stage III, because in stage I weight is thought to be equivalent to volume or "bigness" and is not dissociated from it and attributed to the quality of diverse substances until level IIA. In level IIB the subject comes close to the idea of density with the hypothesis that the object is more or less "filled up," but still in a semimacroscopic way. Finally, when weight and volume are related, which takes place in stage III, the idea of "tight" is presupposed but on a corpuscular scale. Now, from the point of view of space, the idea of "tight" undoubtedly implies the idea of the continuum interior to the surfaces, which up to now were judged primarily according to their perimeter, and especially to the volumes, that is, the consideration of the "whole" and no longer only disconnected partitions.[3] Let us remember, moreover, that to end up with equal weights when one has substances of different densities—for instance, light wax and heavy clay or sand and millet—the subjects of stage I construct equal quantities or even bigger ones for heavier substances, whereas in level IIA the problem is solved. On the other hand, when the child has thus succeeded in building up a piece of clay to the same weight as a cork, it is not until age 9 to 10 (level IIB) that he deduces from it that to obtain the weight of half of the cork it is enough to divide his clay ball in two! In this case we understand the difficulties of distributivity (see § 12), the present problem being distinctly easier.

On the other hand, it is only in stage III that the subjects understand pressure as well as the connections between weight and

[2] See J. Piaget and B. Inhelder, *Le développement des quantités physiques chez l'enfant,* 3rd ed., expanded, ch. VII and IX.

[3] Without doubt there is also an associativity and a commutativity, more difficult to maintain on the corpuscular scale than on the macroscopic level.

lengths, anticipating the idea of time, while the corresponding explanations are to be looked for, as we shall see, in the direction of work. Pressure stems naturally from weight-action, but in terms of a weight-quantity made relative to the surface. The intuitions that now appear validate the idea, up to this point without foundation, that the action of the weight varies with its position. Briefly, each of these actions of relating weight and spatial dimension simply amounts to taking into account its quantity and defining more accurately its diffuse or concentrated action—or its point or extent of application—which therefore implies in all these cases a coordination between weight-quantity and weight-action.

As for the structure of these actions of relating, they all amount, and that is characteristic of stage III, to constructing relationships from relationships, therefore to attributing to objects operations carried out on operations since there is, on the one hand, weight as an operator or as a quantified source of action and, on the other, the determination of its momentary zone of application evaluated in terms of lengths, surfaces, or volumes. Therein lies a causal structuring comparable to the composition of vectors, with the difference that it is no longer a question of coordinating the intensity of the forces with their possible multiple directions but rather with the sectors of space where their actions are localized, whether they start from them or whether they end there. Now, to the degree that, in stage III, the bodies are understood to be made up of particles, these particles determine the relationships with space, whether they are arranged in a more or less tight form (density) or whether they ensure the cohesiveness between the parts of the object, the one that exerts weight (pressure) or the one on which weight is exerted (moment). Therefore, in such cases there certainly intervene two kinds of operations coordinated with each other even though appearing on different levels.

17. The Concept of Work

When it comes to the displacement of a force, work takes place at the point of junction between vectoral compositions and the relationships we have just discussed, of weight with spatial dimensions. The difference is that in work these are two forces: one that is displaced (passive force) and one that is used to displace it (active force). Since they are equivalent, the physicist can measure work by means of one (the result obtained) or the other (the necessary expenditure), but psychologically, the distinction is necessary and we can maintain that the concept of work is developed only once this equivalence is understood. More precisely, work is carried out by a transfer or a transformation of energy from one form to another. However, we shall postpone the examination of this concept to § 18.

R81, quoted in § 16 for the "moment," provided a first sounding on work. Given a four-step stairway, how many plugs must a crane carry to the first step in order to provide work equivalent to the transportation of only one on the fourth step? The subjects of level I judge the work carried out by the height alone or, alternatively, by the number of plugs and the height but without synthesis. In stage II there are attempts at compensation, but with no success in measurement, and it is not until stage III that there is a numerical solution.

R42, already quoted in § 10, took up again the preceding problem on a horizontal plane, transportation of weights by a truck, and on a vertical plane, with a crane, but by measuring the active force by means of the number of gasoline cans used by the truck or the crane. In level IIA the subjects still take into account only weights, neglecting the distances covered, or vice versa. In level IIB there are qualitative or additive compensations, with the same for vertical and horizontal planes. For example, if a can of gas is sufficient to move a plug up to the fourth box on a horizontal plane, it will take 1½ cans for two plugs; two plugs on the first step are equivalent to one plug on the third, etc. It is again only in stage III that metric proportions come into the picture. Repetition of the problem of the staircase gave the same results as in R33.

R82 deals with reduction in terms of three pulleys of different sizes (*A* five times greater than *B* and eight times greater than *C*, all three attached to the same axis), with two main problems. If we hang three equal weights at the same height by means of three strings on the same side of the three pulleys and we make the axis turn, will they go up together, or will one arrive ahead of the others? If two equal weights are held by the same string at the same height on opposite sides of two of the pulleys, what will happen if we let the axis turn? Then, after observing it, why does the weight of the big wheel go down? And why is equilibrium reached for a weight in *A* only by five in *B* and by eight in *C?* In stage I no explanation is given. In level IIA the rise of the three weights is still poorly predicted, but clearly explained by relating the size of the circumferences to the lengths of the strings. On the other hand, the problem of equilibrium is definitely not understood, the subject referring only to the power of the wheels, as if the wheel *A* pulled down the weight hanging from it instead of the weight's turning the wheel. In level IIB the rise is in general clearly predicted and always well explained, but regarding equilibrium, the child presupposes an action made up of the hanging weight and the weight of the wheel (the downward movement in *A* being due to the two together). In stage III, finally, the movements of weights, when the question of equilibrium arises, are related to the size of the circumferences, implying a relationship between work and the displacement of a weight. To estimate the number of weights in *C* balancing a single weight in *A,* it is sufficient, for example, to "see how many times the perimeter of *C* goes into *A*'s."

For its part, R83 deals with reduction in terms of the number of pulleys or of strings. We show the subjects a string in the form of ∧ and then of ∧∨ , with mobile bases, then a double vertical string, and finally a quadruple vertical string pulled by an oblique string. The problems are to predict the displacements and the speeds, then the relationships between weights that are subsequently hooked to the bases. In stage I there is no systematic solution. In level IIA the pull on the left string of ∧ gives an exact prediction of the displacements on the right, but the same is not true for ∧∨—after observation the explanations refer only to the lengths of the strings. There is no consideration of weights. In level IIB, on the other hand, the duplications of the strings intervene, with, consequently, a heavier weight on the single string, on the left, to balance the one on the right. Finally, in stage III proportionality is reached, and reduction is explained by the quality of the works accomplished in terms of the number of strings.

Finally, R84, among other things, deals with a rotating disc on which the child is standing, the speed of which increases or decreases according to whether the subject folds his arms or spreads them out. In stage I the reactions are neither regular nor free of contradictions, and in stage II the explanation is based on the weight, which is supposed to vary with the positions. Stage III, however, is characterized by relating an invariant weight to "a bigger turn" or "a longer run," and therefore by recourse to a concept of the family of work.

The problems to which the concept of work gives rise are the why of its explanatory value and the nature of its operational composition. In the first instance we note, in comparing work with time, that they can be amenable to the same formulation: df for moment (measured, for example, in meters-kilograms) and fd for work (measured in kilograms-meters), but with this essential difference that in df the term d is a static length and in fd it is a course traveled.[1] Now, when we place 1 kg on a balance bar 30 cm from the center, and 3 kg at 10 cm from the center, the subjects of level IIB will definitely succeed in discovering that the relationship weight $\times$ length, providing a condition of equilibrium and will thus succeed in establishing the law of times. They will not, however, understand the reason why. On the other hand, if we move the arms of the balance, the subjects of stage III will find an explanation for this law by noting that in this case the 3-kg weight is raised only a little, whereas the 1-kg weight is raised three times as much. The "work" being the same, $3 \times 1 = 1 \times 3$, we seem to have a better understanding from the sole fact that it is a question of two actions and no longer simply of the static relationship weight $\times$ length. To put it another way, the objects by moving "do" something, which at this stage they continue to "do" in the immobile state, but in the form of "virtual work." There is more than anthropomorphism involved, because it is the substitution of operations for simple relationships that, in general, allows the law to be completed with a causal explanation by bringing to light the transformations themselves.

The structure of the concept of work flows from what precedes, provided we remember that displacing a force presupposes another as a motor. That is why we cannot yet speak of work when the

[1] Not to mention the cases where the cosine is other than one by including the horizontal displacement of a weight in the notions of the "family of work."

subjects of stage II in R82 understand that a big wheel pulls up a weight hung by a string faster than a little wheel, because this string winds around a bigger circumference. On the other hand, we know that they have the concept when they predict that a weight on a big wheel is sufficient to put in balance several weights on smaller wheels, or to pull them up if they remain below a certain weight, because in these cases one force displaces another according to different distances traveled. Likewise, in R42, it is the relationship between the gas cans and the weights moved to varying distances that constitutes the index of the understanding of work.

Briefly, if the compositions examined in § 16 of weight and spatial dimensions already include relationships of relationships and, consequently, through the intervention of the corpuscular scale, operations on operations, there are even more of them in the utilization of the concept of work. There is first the composition of a force and a displacement, considered in its length and often in its direction, therefore equivalent to vectors in psychological complexity. Moreover, there is also a composition between this relationship, which is already at the second power, and the active force making possible the displacement of the passive one. Thus, we have a connection at the third power, which is why its understanding is delayed.

But there is still more, and because the three terms of the composition (the active and passive forces and the displacement produced by the first force) are by nature dynamic, we come closer to a more advanced concept. Physically, work results from a change in the form of energy, and in the case of gas cans, as in R42, it is obviously a question of energy. Psychologically, it is difficult to find a criterion for the appearance of this concept of energy, and it is clear that, in the transmission of an impulse (§ 4), the child will not get to the relationship $\frac{1}{2}mv^2$ any more than the Cartesians did. On the other hand, we shall see in § 18 an example of a transmission of powers distinct from that of movements which will bring us closer to the idea of energy. The concept of work, understood as we have just explained as the action in a spatio-temporal succession of one force on another, is not far from such a transmission, at least in situations of reduction (R82 and 83).

18. The Exchange of Active and Passive Roles and the Concept of Energy

Since it is in stage III that, in general, thinking can handle hypotheses operationally or the possible and the virtual physically, it is evident that the subjects at this level will rapidly distinguish "what we can do" from "what we do," as one of them put it in Aristotelian language. But this distinction of the power from the act is still far from implying a concept of energy, and indicates only a recognition of the fact that a force exists not only in a state of movement but that it continues to act at rest or has the potential to do so. On the other hand, the following data raise a new problem.

R85 deals with a set of two pendulums, made up of balls *A* and *B* held by strings *a* and *b,* the strings being tied together at two thirds of their height by a horizontal elastic. We ask the subjects to predict what will happen if we move ball *A* aside and let it go. Then we conduct the experiment up to the time when the movement of *B* increases and that of *A* decreases, and we ask them to predict and explain what follows. Then comes a second observation, when *A* is set in motion again and *B* slows down, which we ask them to explain and predict what will follow, etc. In level IA the role the strings play is not understood. In level IB it is recognized after observation, with out any necessary sequential order in the actions, but the reactivation of *A* is explained by the fact that this ball "starts up again" as though each could become active again independently of the other. In level IIA there is a prediction and an explanation of the transmission from *A* to *B,* but the reverse is not predicted. Once noted, it is explained by a reciprocal transmission. In level IIB the latter is anticipated, but without continuation of the process. In level IIIA anticipation improves, and in level IIIB (a few subjects from age 12;8 to 15) the whole process is predicted and explained before any observation is made.

The difficulty of the problem resides in the presence of three reversibilities, the first of which is particularly complex. These three reversibilities are (1) the oscillations of a single movement of the pendulum, *A* or *B;* (2) the oscillations of two movements in opposite directions, *A* and *B* crossing each other when their speeds are equal; and (3) the exchange of roles in the transmission, since *A* at first draws *B* along with a weakening of its own movement, and then *B* draws *A* along in turn, etc. In this respect it is striking to see subjects 12 to 15 years old predict this alternating of the active and passive roles of each ball, when most adults who are not physicists do not think of it.

It is this alternation of the active and passive roles of each of the two balls that authorizes us, when it is predicted and understood before any experimenting, to speak of a new mode of transmission, distinct from that of the movement or of the impulse (§ 4). It is true that, in physics, the explanation can be provided strictly in terms of "pulling" and "pushing" and that, if it is easier to couch it in the language of interchanges of energy, the energy also intervenes in the facts of § 4. However, from the point of view of the operations of the subject who is not a physicist, these phenomena can be much less easily assimilated than the transmissions of § 4. Indeed, what is transmitted here is no longer a simple push, since when one of the balls slows down its oscillations the other increases its own, not just once but in alternating reciprocities. What is acquired by the ball that becomes passive is a power and no longer a movement: It is the power to become active in turn. It is therefore possible to see in it the emergence of a new concept and, even if the subject does not use the word "energy," to call it that since we are talking about an operator at a higher level, belonging particularly to substage IIIB.

Naturally, this does not mean that the subjects of this substage will generalize the concept and will see henceforth in the transmission of the movement a composition $\frac{1}{2}mv^2$ being added to mv. It does mean that, in some situations, the subject arrives at complex compositions, and we have seen that he is not far from it in connection with work in reduction. Even more, we know that kinetic energy $\frac{1}{2}mv^2$ is equivalent to the work fd brought about by accelerating the mass m starting from rest, and it is therefore striking, from the genetic point of view, to see these two concepts of work and energy being developed at the same level in different experimental situations. However, in the present case, where no quantification yet occurs, contrary to that of reduction, we do not have the impression of an operational *schème* constructed in advance in the logico-mathematical field and then attributed to relationships between physical objects, except in what concerns general but alternating reciprocity ascribed to the balls. It seems that we are, on the contrary, faced with a situation in which the physical problem includes unforeseen relationships that must be structured at the time of their discovery.

19. Heat and Light

In §§ 4–18 we were concerned only with cases of mechanical causality. These are particularly within reach of the child, with continuous progress from levels IA to IIB and sometimes with even some precocious successes, because they correspond to causal actions by so-called manipulations. The collaboration of the motor powers of the hand and visual control undoubtedly explains the special character of the mechanism through these direct links with the action itself. However, the material activities of the subject clearly include many other dimensions. Vision can function alone independently of manual actions, sound plays a continuous role in social as well as physical exchanges, the subject is conscious of his thermal perceptions as soon as he is hot or cold, without having to speak of contacts with heated or frozen bodies, burns, etc. But apart from the direction of the look, the actions relative to temperature and the control of the voice, or attention when it is a question of listening better or not at all, these diverse behaviors give rise only to controls that are much less active and extensive than manual or sensori-motor activities in general. More particularly, they do not lead to an awareness of the intimate mechanisms of the retina, of thermal equilibrium, or of vocal cords as they do in the muscular action of the limbs, where we can distinguish, when needed, each different movement of the arms, hands, or fingers. It is therefore important to examine what elementary experiments in these fields yield from the point of view of causality.

R86 gave us the first indications of the concepts of the transmission of heat by means of a steel ball heated in the presence of the subject and then dipped in cold water, or of a cold ball dipped in hot water, with an ice cube as a control. In these situations, even though transmission is immediate, the subjects of stage I refuse to admit that the heat "passes" from the ball into the water or the reverse even though they predict heating and cooling; they think that both are due to a kind of contagious action, which is not a transmission in the sense of a displacement in space. A third of the 6-year-old subjects thus admit that the hot ball will heat the water, but will not itself cool, and we again find such affirmations with two subjects out of ten, age 7 to 8, and one out of ten, age 11 to 12. For the others (more than half up to about age 11), there will be a complete exchange, often with repeated alternations, without equalization. As for equalization, it is not admitted until stage II and only then by a fourth (age 7 to 8) and a third (age 9 to 10) of the subjects. We must wait almost until stage III for the effects to be simultaneous and continuous.

R87 then dealt with conductibility for the purpose of sharpening the ideas of transmission. With a candle we heated the end of a glass tube or an aluminum strip so that pieces of wax melted at the other end. In stage I it is the flame that passes through the hole in the tube or along the metal to reach the wax. In stage II heat and fire become progressively differentiated, but not radiation and conduction. Only in stage III is conduction understood.

R88 took up again the problems of water, this time using a receptacle in two compartments separated by a movable glass partition in which we put equal or unequal (double) quantities of warm and cold water, or warm and "very hot" water. In stage I there are neither transmissions nor quantifications. In stage II as well, there is no free transmission through the glass partition. Six subjects out of 29 admit a semitransmission in the form of influences (radiation). When we put in the compartments equal and *a fortiori* unequal quantities of warm water of the same temperature, taken out of the same thermos in full view of the child, three-fourths of the subjects still think that the resultant will be warmer, as though the increase in the quantity of liquid entails that of heat. It is not until stage III that there is transmission *per se* and valid quantifications.

We thus see the considerable difference between these reactions and those that concern the transmission of movement. In stage I there is not even any immediate transmission, as if the passage of heat were equivalent to a unilateral action without any loss, like the influences that one living being can exert on another without thereby losing his powers. After an intermediate stage II, it is only in stage III that the mediate transmission is understood, even though purely internal transmissions, in the case of movement, are already grasped. There is therefore a lag of an entire stage between the two kinds of ideas. The reason for this could be that the causal model from which come the problems of heat is an irreversible, probabilistic mixture and no longer a reversible model, but we know that in its simple, noncombinatory forms, such as mixtures of beads starting with unconnected collections, this probabilistic model is within reach starting with stage II. Therefore, the lag still exists, and in order to judge its nature we must examine the problems of light.

Among other things, R89 deals with vision and the nature of the image in a mirror or of the light cast by a lamp. For almost all the subjects vision is a passage from the eye to the object and not the reverse, except when nothing passes, as is the case with small children. In the case of a flashlight, the majority of the older ones admit an action of the flashlight on the eye, but we find the problem again in R91, and many subjects continue to believe in a passage from the eye to the lamp. As far as the mirror is concerned, there is no reflection in stage I, while, starting with age 7 to 8, the mirror sends back the image or the light in the form of "reflections." But when we place behind the child an object he can see in the mirror, the most frequent solution is that of a passage from the eye to the mirror and from there to the object, but in some cases, of a meeting in the mirror between what leaves the eye and what leaves the object.

R90 used a box with polaroid panes capable of multiplying colors. In stage I the colors become a substance in the form of material emanations of the objects, like shadows at the same level, capable of hiding, of reappearing and of "fading" but without the possibility of going very far. In stage II the colors constitute "reflections" capable of being produced anywhere, but without specifying their mode of passage. In stage III, on the other hand, there is added the reflection of daylight and a search for compositions.

Finally, R91 deals with the transmission of light and heat in connection with a lamp throwing a circle of light on a screen either close or far away. Up to level IIB there is no transmission, but some kind of action at a distance. In stage I the quantity of light is a function of the size of the circle, which is predicted as decreasing with distance. When the facts show that the largest circle is the farthest away, the subjects of level IB do not hesitate to attribute to it more light, but without transmission in the sense of a displacement in space and by specifying that there is "nothing" between the lamp and the screen. In the intermediate level IIA, the same thing is true concerning this last point, but the contradiction is sensed, though not raised; in IIB, however, the inverse connection between the quantity of light and the distance finally wins out, and the subject begins to use kinematic expressions such as the light "leaves," "comes straight forward," etc. In level IIIA the transmission becomes explicit, but the enlargement of the circle at a distance is still poorly explained. Finally, in level IIIB the subject suggests a cone of light with a widening of rays in terms of the distance, the largest surface of the circle being consonant with a decrease in the quantity of light.

Therefore, we note that, despite the daily use of flashlights and the common ideas on "rays" of the sun or of sources of light, the understanding of the transmission of light is scarcely more precocious than that of heat. It is not until stage III that the subject admits the existence of a light "between the machine (lamp of R91) and the round spot . . . I don't see it but I know it is there." In the transmissions of movement "through" the marbles of R2 (see § 4), the subject does not see anything go through and notes only the final result. He still deduces from it, starting with level IIA, the necessary existence of a semi-internal passage of this movement, while, for light as well as for heat, we must wait until level III for purely internal transmissions in order to have a passage as a displacement and not as a kind of immediate although distant action. We could, indeed, bring up the possible effects of lighting or heating techniques. We flick on an electric light switch and the light shines, etc. But these techniques ought to lead to the idea of mediate transmission. We speak of "current," etc. In the case of transmission of movements, the subjects who want to indicate a passage inside the marbles sometimes speak of "electricity" to designate a flux and as a synonym of what others call precisely "current." Why, therefore, is there none of this in answer to our questions?

The hypothesis that seems to emerge is that the attribution of the operations to the objects, therefore the success of causal explanations, especially in the field of transmissions, is a function of the causal action of the subject himself and of the quality of the active controls or material regulations that ensure their success. In this case the attribution of transitivity, of additive compositions, of compensations with reversible direction, etc., is facilitated, in the mechanical realm, by the richness of the visually controlled manual behaviors, therefore of actions already causal but that, by their coordination, play in other respects an important role in the genesis of operations. On the other hand, this is not so in the case of heat or light, and it is not the fact of learning how to turn on radiators or switch on electric lights that helps when it comes to understanding structures or even transmissions relative to these segments of physical reality.

20. Sound and Air

Even though air plays a role in the transmission of sound, starting with stage II, we do not because of that associate here the two problems, which would be quite artificial. We do it because if, as we have just assumed, the attribution of operations to objects depends on the wealth and the regulation of the causal actions of the subject, which constitute the area of interference between his ideas on objective connections and his own operations, then air occupies an especially interesting intermediary position between solids and liquids, which can be manipulated, and realities such as heat, light, and sound, which cannot, on the scale of their structural compositions. That is why a somewhat systematic examination of the ideas relating to air can provide us, in a final analysis, with a retrospective picture of connections or absence of connections between mechanical causality and the other forms of structuring. But let us begin with sound.

R89, part of which deals with hearing, shows that, in level IA, nothing goes from the object to the ear: "Does noise (we tap on the table) go toward your ears?" "No." "Does it make a path?" "It stays there." "Do some people say that it's coming toward our ears?" "That is false" (6;10). Starting with level IB, noise goes to the ear, but in general returns to its source as an emanation from the object returning to it. In stage II it goes in straight lines in all directions and, as we approach stage III, it is a "tapping" that "rings," etc., and that spreads through the intermediary of air, if it is not itself air.

R92 takes up again the problem by means of a sound produced by a dangling needle when it is hit by another needle. In level IA the sound stays in the needle and moves around inside it. In level IB it reaches the ears but, with most of the subjects, it then goes back into the needle. In stage II it is a shaking that spreads throughout by means of the air. In stage III air itself becomes capable of vibrating and thus of transmitting the sound.

R93 used an apparatus with two strings stretched differently, the segments of which can vary in lengths in order to produce sounds of different pitches. The relationship of sound with length, Pythagoras' law, is discovered in the different questions asked, in stage II and especially in level IIB but, except for stage III, where the length and the tension are disassociated, the explanations provided suggest only the tension as a factor of a mechanical nature more easily understood, length taking on meaning only in the wave motion hypothesis.

We thus note that the transmission of sound poses much less difficulty than that of light and heat. In this respect we should remember that, for the subjects of stage I, we think with the voice. When we ask the child to close his mouth and tell us if he can still think, we sometimes get answers of the type: "It's my little mouth in the back of my head which talks to my mouth in front." Since the mouth is used in breathing, there is thus established a close connection between speech and air, or even between thought and breath—we are quite familiar with the use of the term breath for soul in ancient tongues. Since speech constitutes a behavior that is socialized much more and much earlier than sight, since we exchange sounds more than visual or thermal impressions, it is no longer a question of a single subject centered on his own action, but of a continuous communication between diverse sources of sound. It is difficult not to see a psychomorphic influence of this situation in the reactions of young subjects thinking that sounds exist in the objects even when they are not heard, then going only into the ears and nowhere else in order to go back to their source. Finally, the sounds are precociously linked to air, which can be inside as well as outside the individuals in question.

From the point of view of causality, air is definitely the most polyvalent idea used by the young subjects, even more so than that of weight and perhaps even preceding it.

> From the age of 2;11 a little girl, who was observed every day, attributed the waves of the lake to the wind and the wind to trees. At 4;6 she has the wind play the role of displacing the moon, after which she pushes the air with her hand in the opposite direction and blows twice: "Now the moon is big, because of air, it is now blown up." After many remarks of the same kind, at 5;6 she has babies born from an air bubble coming out of the mother's stomach. At 5;8 she whirls around until dizzy and thinks that everything around her starts to move "by hand"; that is, a breeze is made with the movements of the hand or of the entire body. Then she makes a distinction between the transparent or "the white by hand" and the "blue by hand" of the sky, which the height of her father reaches and which explains why for him nothing seems to move. In short, air serves to explain any phenomenon whose cause is obscure.
>
> In R72, some subjects age 6 to 11 use air to explain the rise of water in a narrow tube by capillary action. Let us quote a child of 6;2: "We could say that it is like a straw (used for a soft drink): when you blow, it goes up." And at 9;6: the air "draws up the water." "How?" "The air is in the whole tube. When we make it go down the air pushes the water up." On the other hand, this does not work with oil, because "the air cannot go down under to raise it up." In other words, for these two subjects to suck up consists of pushing up from below.
>
> R11, already cited in § 4, shows that in stage I the force of attraction of a magnet depends on a "glue" that also has the power to "blow" and "make a breeze" when there is repulsion. In stage II

air no longer intervenes, except sometimes in the guise of "air from the magnet" which is its current or the force that "attracts."

On the other hand, R94 is concerned exclusively with air, dealing with the mechanism of a big syringe and, as often happens when air plays an effective causal role in an apparatus, it is recognized only later on. In stage I there is no air in the syringe because, up to stage II, air does not exist in the immobile state. When you try to push the piston down to the end, since the syringe is plugged up, the subjects of stage I "feel" the resistance but attribute it to the fact that the glass is tightening up, without any evidence, especially if we close the upper opening, while if we open it, the glass "stretches out." At level IIA air is suggested following observations, but it is then endowed with contradictory powers: Either it helps the piston go down or else it pushes it back by "fighting" it. In level IIB air is referred to from the outset; it pushes the piston back because, when moved to where it does not want to be, "it wants to come back," etc. Therefore, in stages IIA and IIB, air already exists in the immobile state, but it acts only in motion, without the subjects thinking of pressure. The concept of pressure is understood only in stage III. The compressed air pushes back the piston and, if we pull it up without unplugging the base of the syringe, some subjects understand the effect of the vacuum as a suction device and the necessity for a given quantity of air to occupy a normal and constant volume.

R95 deals with a kind of water manometer. We blow into a tube going through a glass jar, the bottom of which is filled with water. The water then rises into another tube and goes down again when there is no pressure. In stage I the subject does not predict the rise of the water under the influence of the air. Upon observation, the air moves the water along as it goes through it. In stage II the air pushes the water but still goes through it a little bit. A piece of paper placed on the second tube is blown away by air, and the subject continues to wonder whether or not it is the same air as was blown into the first tube, which is accepted in stage I. In stage III the mechanism is understood. Air accumulates on the water, and its pressure displaces it.

R96 used a "ludion," a toy made by a tube placed vertically in a bottle three-quarters full of water. If we put a stopper on the bottle, the air pressure causes some water to enter a little opening at the bottom of the tube, which then goes down while, if we uncork the flask, the tube goes up. In stage I the air plays no role. The stopper or the water have powers sufficient to explain everything. In level IIA air plays a necessary role, but with contradictory effects as in R94. It helps the tube go down, then makes it go up, etc. In level IIB it is limited to pushing toward the bottom, but the pressure accompanying a decrease in volume does not intervene until level IIIA. The level IIIB subjects, moreover, understand that the air causes some water to enter through the bottom of the tube.

R97 studied the answers to the simple question of knowing why two holes are necessary for liquid to flow from a tin can. In stage I a single hole suffices, and air plays no role. In level IIA it intervenes, but with the customary polyvalence. It comes out of the water or comes from outside, goes away so that the water has room to go out, mixes with it to help it, floats or penetrates it, etc. In level IIB it acquires the precise function of pushing the water, but in the form of a current with variable directions in relation to the liquid, making it come out again with or after it. Finally, in stage III, air takes the place of the liquid, which comes out alone.

Let us recall that in R63 (jet-propelled balloon, §14), the air that leaves the balloon through the back can, in level IB, take off in any direction and make an about-face to push the balloon in the other direction. In level IIA it can be divided with one section facing in one direction and the other in the opposite direction. It is not until level IIB that its direction is stabilized, the return being due to its bouncing off walls.

R98 used a light paper cylinder the top of which is lit. The hot air, which rises as the paper burns, is replaced by cold air descending into the cylinder, which then floats away almost burned. In stage I this flight is due to the paper, which is "flying," to the fire, to the wind, etc. In stage II the subject suggests the presence of air or of "heat" in or under the paper to explain the flight, the air being able to come from the outside, from inside the paper, or even being produced by its movements during the burning. But the necessity for cylindrical form is not understood until stage III, where the cold air goes down in the cylinder by replacing the hot air which rises.

R99 replaced the cylinder with a paper spiral, which we whirl around a rod above a source of heat. In stage I the candle or the immobile axis explains everything. In level IIA air is introduced, making the paper "turn" or "rise," as in the helicoidal tube mentioned in § 13, without following a determined direction. In level IIB it pushes the spiral by creating a current that follows its contours. Finally, in stage III the role of the slope of the paper is understood as a condition for an effective push.

In R100, hot air makes a propeller turn. The role of the angle of the blades is understood starting with level IIB, doubtless because of the horizontal plane on which the propeller turns as opposed to the preceding spiral. In level IA there is no intermediary between the candle and the movement of the propeller. In level IB, heat and smoke are suggested. In level IIA air is brought up, but without any other mention, and in IIB the curved form of the blades becomes necessary.

In order to trace a regular development from such disparate facts, we must first note that, during stage I, air is constantly mentioned in situations in which it is not involved, and it plays a role of a kind of *deus ex machina* to account for phenomena otherwise difficult to explain, but, in the eyes of the subject, it does not intervene in circumstances in which, in fact, it exercises a causal action. The reason for this is that in stage I air does not yet constitute a permanent substance that continues to exist in the immobile state (on the other hand, in R92, sound still remains in the needle even when it is not heard). It acquires reality only when in motion, as if by a series of creations *ex nihilo,* like that air supposedly produced by the hand movements of the little girl age 5;8 mentioned at the beginning of the preceding data. Surely, starting with stage I, air has the power of pushing, which is objectively correct, but with the considerable difference that the air pushing an object has often been produced by the spontaneous movements of the object itself, which is a primitive form of ἀντιπερίσταδις (antiperistasis). We have an example of it in R98, when the paper that burns flies away because of the air produced by its own movements. We have previously cited many examples: trees, waves, dust, clouds, etc., which produce wind by moving and are then activated by their own wind. But in addition to these pushes, which are frequently auto-pushes, air serves for anything. It draws along, it sucks in (on this point see the confusions in R72 between sucking in and pushing up from below, even in the case of a drinking straw), it attracts the "ludion" as well as repels it, it can result from the "glue" of the magnet when it "blows" to produce a repulsion, it retraces its steps to push the balloon in

R63, it crosses the water and directs it anywhere, it makes the moon grow big by blowing it up and even at times brings babies into the world, etc. On the other hand, just when it effectively plays a role in the immobile state or even sometimes in motion, it is not mentioned, as in R94, where the subjects of stage I explain the resistance encountered by the piston by imagining displacements of the glass, R95, R96, R97, R99, and R100, when air is completely absent just when its action is almost evident.

From this situation, in which air is only a spontaneous and momentary force or power, how then does the subject, during stage II, go on to the idea of a substance continuing to exist in the immobile state or set in motion by other bodies, which are no longer the source of it but only a cause of displacement, acting only by pushes or pulls? Since the air is invisible and its directions are not observable except indirectly through the intermediary of the effects obtained, this change of attitude becomes even more of a problem because there is a very regular evolution from levels IIA to IIB (R94, R96, R97, R63, R99, and R100). In IIA the air pushes or pulls, but its directions remain contradictory and its points of application poorly identified, while in IIB the directions are correct on the whole and the process of pushing is analyzed when needed, that is, rebound in R63, blades of the propellers in R100. Of course, when there is progress like this in understanding, it can only be a question of the attribution of operations to the object-air: conservation and motor transitivity in level IIA, and the beginnings of a geometrization of directions, systems of coordinates, in level IIB. Finally, in stage III there appear as usual the notions of pressure and of volume occupied in connection with the operations already encountered. But on what indices or experimental facts can such attributions be founded? In the case of solids and even of liquids, the progress of the mechanism is linked to all kinds of effective causal actions as well as to the development of the operations of the subject. In the case of air, on the other hand, we see only these operations at work. Yet, would they have the power to modify so profoundly the physical interpretations of air without an experimental contribution correlative and interdependent with this structuring? This contribution seems to exist, but it is not due to a direct manipulation of the air itself.

It appears evident that it is by a constant assimilation of this single case with the whole of causal structures constructed in the field of solids and liquids that the ideas on air are transformed. In other words, it is rather the general coherence of the system of notions and physical operations that here plays the decisive role, and not a local construction. If we dare risk this comparison, there is even in it some analogy with the manner in which physicists formerly came to specify in detail the properties and actions of ether in correspondence with the facts otherwise known, with the difference that air exists and that its effects are perceptible.

On the whole, despite the fact that air does not follow the usual pattern, it plays a quite considerable role in the development of causality as an attribution of operations to objects. At first a quasimagic power linked to a substance existing only occasionally but produced by the actions of the subject and by those of bodies in motion, air is then mechanized, after a delay, because of its mixed origins, but, finally, successfully, as it is brought into the vast process of operational structuring from which it cannot escape, not because of particular discoveries it has brought about, but by virtue of analogies or rather general deductive requirements that it cannot avoid.

Conclusions

At the end of this introduction we believe that we have reached part of the stated goal: to interpret this surprising combination of production and conservation that every variety of causality includes by virtue of the analogous characteristics presented by the broad outlines of operational composition, to the extent that these structures of operations would be attributed and not simply applied to objects, therefore, to the extent that the objects would constitute operators functioning like those of our reason, which would make their actions comprehensible.

It goes without saying that these analogies or even isomorphisms, such as groups, of general characteristics mean neither identity nor even isomorphism in specifics between a particular causal relationship and a given operation. Later (paragraph VI) we shall return to these differences. However, what is remarkable is that we find again in the causal structures some necessary forms of operational composition, such as transitivity (see § 4), reversibility and symmetries (§ 6), additivity (§§ 7–8), multiplicativity with proportions and distributivity (§§ 9–12), the composition of inversions and reciprocities (§ 14), sufficient reason (§ 15),[1] the coordinations of actions with spatial dimensions (§§ 16–17), and the alternation of roles between operators (§ 18). We even note how the notions derived from actions of the subject, without sufficiently active control to translate them into mechanical connections, are finally integrated into the whole system (§§ 19–20).

If the definition of causality as an attribution of operations to objects remains in the current tradition of rationalism, the interesting thing in the parallelisms observed is that they force us to find again in the very development of these causal explanations the necessary combination of these two components of every operational composition, which production and conservation are, since one of the two is generally overestimated at the expense of the other. In other words, in the preceding facts, the emphasis must be placed not on the attribution of particular operational kinds or aspects, but on that of compositions as such, in their two inseparable characteristics of transformation and coherence.

However, if such a natural relationship exists between causality and operations, which would mean that both adhere to the laws of reality and therefore to the common roots of the subject and objects, then why so much work and so many difficulties until their discovery or their conscious realization? Why this long

---

[1] To these general forms of operational organization attributed to objects we can add recurrence. The latter is implicit and remains especially "applied" in the case of transmissions in general and particularly in the blockings of Vergnaud (R13). Its role is evident in a new study which is part of a group of studies of action. Dominoes are placed vertically close to each other in such a way that the fall of the first on the second produces one after the other the fall of the whole series. In this case it is clear that the casual relationship between n and $n + 1$ is generalized for every case starting with 1 and $1 + 1$ and permits retroactive reconstitutions as well as anticipations. Recurrence is then attributed to the objects themselves, and does not constitute merely an operation internal to the reasonings of the subject.

evolution in psychogenesis, the steps of which we have just re-traced? Why these initial confusions, sources of errors and of ignorance, between the subject and objects, since at the end of their conflict they eventually coordinate their actions and even discover that they are profoundly convergent? These are the broad outlines of this dialectic made up of undifferentiations, oppositions and mutual deformations, then of differentiations and coordinations that have yet to be traced. We can very briefly characterize them as follows: common origins in the action but with, from the outset, a predominant influence of particular actions for causality and general coordinations for the logical connections between *schèmes;* undifferentiation still very persistent in stage I, with positive sol-idarities, but also with mutual deformations between the causal and preoperational aspects of thought; partial differentiations in stage II with coordinations only where there are differentiations; differentiation and coordination in constant progress in stage III.

(I) As for common origins, there is no longer any need for lengthy commentaries. Every sensori-motor action is causal in its psychophysiological mechanism and in its results on objects, since it amounts to using them materially by displacing them, linking them together, etc. However, none of these particular actions re-mains exclusively causal, since by being repeated, by being gen-eralized, by being connected with others, etc., it becomes part of the continuous construction of a schematism dominated by the re-quirements of a general coordination, this second aspect of ac-tions providing the basis for future operations of intelligence. At the outset, therefore, there are both a close connection between the causal aspect of actions and the aspect that can be called logical. However, there is also a distinction, which still does not draw a clear-cut line of demarcation, since the simpler the action, the less differences there are between its particular properties stemming more or less from causality and its powers of schematic assimilation, the source of the logical or prelogical activities of the subject. But what is interesting about this initial relative non-dissociation is that it shows a complementarity in the functioning more than confusions in the conscious realization, that realization developing on a different level from that of execution, beginning only with the conceptualization due to the semiotic function, there-fore, in stage I, of representative intelligence.

(II) On the other hand, as far as stage I of representative thought is concerned, the questions of relationships between causality and the preoperational structures arise at the level of conceptualizations, that is, of causal precausal notions on the one hand, and of the prelogical organization of judgments or functions on the other. It is therefore at this level that it is necessary to talk of relative undifferentiation.

This undifferentiation is so important that we can refer to it to answer two fundamental questions raised by the reactions peculiar to this stage. Why do the concepts, inferences, etc., of subjects age 2 to 6 remain preoperational, if not because of illegitimate intrusions of causality and an insufficient causality? And why does this causality remain insufficient and, so to speak, precausal, if not because of the influence of the logical structures of this level which, in turn, remain rudimentary? In short, the hypothesis is that the causal and logical structures of stage I would both feel the slowing-down effects of a relative undifferentiation, whereas a coordination due to a sufficient differentiation would be profitable for them.

Beginning with the general characteristics of reversibility and conservation, which the prelogical structures of this stage lack, we can hardly question that this lack is due primarily to causal action on the deductive operation. When the subject pours a liquid from one container into another, modifies the form of an object or the spatial arrangement of a collection, these actions remain all the more distant from the rule of reversible operations the more they appear to the subject to be of a causal nature, to the extent that causality introduces new effects that are not preformed and that modify the object without our being able in advance to impose limits on these transformations, which will be the case only when this causality becomes an attribution of operations. In other words, since most causal actions are irreversible, for an action to be internalized in an operation it is necessary for it to be sufficiently differentiated from causal actions or from the causal aspect of actions in general; otherwise, undifferentiation will constitute a delaying factor.

As for the inclusion of the part in the whole, a subject, who is in no way exceptional, when asked if, given about 20 wooden beads 15 to 18 of which are brown, the necklace that could be made from the wooden beads would be longer or shorter than that of the brown beads, answered substantially that the brown-bead necklace would be longer because once the brown beads were strung, we would not be able to use them to put them in the other. This is an irrefutable answer if it is a question of synchronized causal actions, but it testifies to the fact that at this level thought still proceeds like material action without the necessary mobility to compare a nondissociated whole *B* to a dissociated part *A,* since the physical act of taking out *A* then makes this part comparable only to its complement *A′.*

Likewise, the difficulties of seriation, proceeding at first only in successive pairs without mediations, or the inability to evaluate numbers or quantities by correspondences other than optical, that is, founded on the spatial arrangement and the length of rows, also show the subordination where reasoning stops in respect to material and causal interlocking.[2] To say that one row of ten discs contains more than another row of ten discs that is a little shorter, is to rely on the same considerations of symmetry or asymmetry that make a ruler placed perpendicular to the edge of a table fall if it extends for more than half of its length beyond the table (see § 6), and to seriate the objects only by pairs reminds one very closely of the transmissions without mediators of the beginnings of causality.[3]

(III) Briefly, we can legitimately suppose that the preoperational character of thought in stage I depends on a lack of sufficient differentiation in the causal connections. But the converse is undoubtedly true and the character, either precausal or of psychomorphic causality, of the physical interpretations peculiar to this stage could not be explained without a relative undifferentiation of the prelogical connections.

[2] Previously, we mentioned in this connection the figurative subordination of number to space, but in addition we have considerations of dimensions, symmetries, etc., in an equally causal sense.

[3] Let us recall again the experiments of Bever and Mehler, in which they thought to prove the existence of a precocious and even "innate" quantification in children age 2 to 3, and which we repeated without finding the same results. It is obvious that every action modifying the given whole appears to the subject to increase the quantity of it as if a causal action could enrich its object only quantitatively.

Of these characteristics the two most general are the difficulties in the control of the words "all" and "some," and the absence of reciprocity in the relationships. If we maintain that these deficiencies in operational compositions are due to the undifferentiation of logical and causal connections, it is evident that the insufficiency of these prelogical structures will, conversely, prevent causality from reaching a rational level. But we wish to go further and show that some prelogical connections are translated directly into rather specific precausal forms. The poorly mastered relationships of "all" and "some," which are difficulties of inclusion, begin, for example, with a situation in which the subject scarcely distinguishes the individual from the collection. "The garden slug" or "a moon" thus mean neither the same individual object nor even the same species, but remain intermediary between the singular and the collective, like a kind of individualization representative of the whole or of exemplarity. When, in the problem of the formation of shadows, the child says that the shadow of a screen produced on the table "is the shade under the trees," or when, to explain the movement of an object, he says that "it is the wind" that pushes it, he will not be able either to decide between the two possibilities "$x = x'$" taken as the same individual object and "x is analogous to x' inasmuch as it belongs to the same class." The result, then, is that he will assert that the shade of the trees or the wind from outside have instantaneously passed through the window to act on the table. All the reasonings by "transduction" are founded on this analogical process, and it occurs frequently in level IA, in the many causal actions without spatial or intelligible contact.

As for the lack of reciprocity of relationships, it plays, likewise, an important role in causality, especially in the difficulties of establishing the necessary connections between a relationship and its converse. For example, if A is placed on B, which is placed on C, the weight that "weighs" in the direction ABC is not the same as that which "is carried" in the direction CBA. All the inequalities in the distance covered by objects pulled by the same string stem from analogous difficulties of composition between relationships, etc.

In general, the combined difficulties of the nesting [*emboîtement*] ("all" and "some") and of the logical composition of the relationships result in an absence of quantification, and this lack constitutes one of the most constant characteristics of causality peculiar to stage I.

In conclusion, the relative undifferentiation between causal or precausal and logical or prelogical connections entails continuous interactions, at the core of which it is possible to discern influences in both directions. It would therefore be somewhat artificial to expect to find at this level operations "applied" or "attributed" to the object, first because there do not yet exist operational forms distinct from direct connections between contents, and therefore no operations, and then because the actions of the subject performed on the objects involve by undifferentiation an assimilation of the responses of the latter to the manipulations of the former, from which comes the psychomorphism. If a complete attribution of the actions of the subject to the object can be ascribed to this psychomorphism, this is a different kind of attribution from the distinct attributions of the application and from that made possible by the formation of operations in stage II after sufficient differentiation of the operational form and the causal content of the actions.

(IV) It is therefore in stage II that this differentiation takes place, but it is still limited, and the first problem is to understand why. Indeed, the operations called "concrete" are only partially dissociated from their content and consist of successive structurings of different contents, with systematic, horizonal lags [*décalages*]. Let us recall, for example, that conservations (with the same three general arguments of identity, reversibility, and compensations), seriations, and transitivities apply to weight only at about age 9, while exactly the same operational forms are used starting with age 7 for the simple quantities of matter. The reason clearly depends on a continuation of the influences of causality on logic, so evident in stage I. It is in terms of its complex, dynamic properties (see § 16) that weight can be logicized only at a later period, etc.

Conversely, if causality itself in stage II does not go beyond certain limits (semi- and not entirely internal transmissions, difficulty of vectoral compositions, etc.), the first reason for it is, of course, that operations, the progress of which is slowed down by the insufficiency of their budding differentiation from causality, cannot in turn promote causality beyond this level. Nevertheless, by being sufficiently differentiated, these operations begin to be organized, and the progress of their coordination permits, as we have seen, not only multiple "applications," identical with the structuring of the contents, therefore with the very organization of these concrete operations, but also a certain number of "attributions" explaining the progress of causality at this stage, such as mediate transmissions, etc. However, a second reason intervenes, which imposes a limit on this progress. This is that the first forms of organization of operations remain rather elementary and at the first power, as opposed to operations on operations, which characterize stage III because of the continuous workings of reflexive abstractions. In fact, these primary operational structures still consist only of "groupings," which are incomplete groups and seminetworks and are still lacking in combinatory logic, and INRC groups with two reversibilities. The result is that, with operational thought thus progressing by "contiguities," step by step, for lack of combinatory logic, causality, arising from its attributions, will likewise recognize only what can be called unilinear sequences in time, that is, successive sequences without multiple and simultaneous interactions, as well as space, that is, privileged directions without vectoral compositions between directions of unequal forces.

We might assume that the step-by-step compositions that limit the mobility of the operational structures of stage II are really due to the delaying influences of causality on operations, that delay being the result of lack of sufficient differentiation and therefore of sufficient coordination. Indeed, the concrete operations bearing directly on objects and the characteristics of these stemming largely from causality could, from this fact, not only delay the structurings, as we have just seen in connection with weight, but also impose on operations their unilinear modes of step-by-step composition. But that is not all, because the passage from operations on objects to operations on operations, which will mark the arrival of stage III, presupposes a continuous construction through reflexive abstraction that does not depend only on the objects concerned but that implies a certain thought activity that cannot be accelerated at will nor in terms of external circumstances alone. It is undoubtedly on that thought activity that the speed of differentiations between causality and operations mainly depends.

(V) Finally, in stage III the differentiation of causality and operations is sufficient to permit both the free progress of the operations and of the rather rich attributions ensuring the equally remarkable development of causality at this level. Up to this point, the evolution of complementary structures such as these remained somewhat paradoxical. On the one hand, we have consistently noted (§§ 4–18) the mutual support that they give each other, the operations furnishing by attributions a deducible form to causality and the physical experience necessary to causality stimulating in other respects the work of the construction of the operations. But, on the other hand, we have just recognized (paragraphs II–IV) that the undifferentiation of these same structures, which is considerable in stage I and still appreciable in stage II, obstructs their development. In fact, there is nothing contradictory in this, because their reciprocal services vary as coordinations presupposing a sufficient differentiation, while the undifferentiation is a source of confusion or deformation.

The examination of stage III seems to confirm for us the sound basis for this interpretation, since it is then that the operations are sufficiently dissociated from their content to be able to function in a formal way and then that the "attributions" to objects of the operations thus refined become responsible for the decisive progress of causality in all the fields studied. It is therefore only at this stage that the subject's thinking begins to resemble functionally scientific thought, the two most striking characteristics of which are the following: (1) a permanent agreement between the intellectual tools of deduction and the experiment, an agreement the banality of which is the less evident since the first are better dissociated and better differentiated than the second; and (2) an uninterrupted series of mutual services that these two kinds of procedures render each other, the most refined experiments forcing new formalized reconstructions and the most abstract theories leading, to the extent that their formal distinctions are most advanced, to new verifications the results of which were until then unforeseeable.

(VI) However, an enigma still remains in the evolution we have just reviewed. If, on the one hand, causality and operations have a common origin in the actions of the subject, with the only difference being that the first depends more on particular actions and the second on their coordinations, and if, on the other hand, these two kinds of structures reinforce each other by their differentiation but oppose each other to the degree that they remain undifferentiated, then of what does this differentiation consist, and how does it proceed?

This problem of going from cognitive structures initially undifferentiated, and thus sources of internal oppositions, to structures both differentiated and coordinated in a coherent way dominates, in reality, the whole mental development in its fundamental processes of progressive equilibration, of periodic disequilibrations and constant reequilibrations. The question of relations between logico-mathematical operations and causality thus constitutes only a particular case, although an especially important one by reason of the great dychotomy that it represents. It is therefore necessary to remember the generality of the problem before characterizing the terms of this particular differentiation.

In all the fields analyzed up to now, at the outset the notions or the undifferentiated structures include, in varying degrees, implicit or even explicit contradictions. For example, the relative undifferentiation of time and speed can lead to judgments of the type "faster = farther = more time," as well as "having arrived faster = less time." The undifferentiation of force and of movement amounts to considering "the impetus" either as the source or as the result of the movements. The weight-action property permits the young subjects to state simultaneously that little boats float because they are light and the water carries them, and that big boats float because they are heavy and can carry themselves.

If such undifferentiations are self-explanatory insofar as they concern concepts drawn or stemming in part from actions themselves poorly analyzed from the two points of view, operational and causal, the motor of the differentiations and especially the reason for their solidarity with coordinations are therefore to be looked for in the dialectic processes that contradictions raise. When these are felt, and it is inevitable that they will be felt sooner or later, the fact alone of looking for and of succeeding *a fortiori* in raising them leads both to distinctions—therefore to a differentiation of notions—and to an effort of coherence—therefore to coordinations. Essentially, these distinctions and this coherence can be obtained only by an "overtaking" [*Aufhebung, dépassement*], consisting of a reshaping and, in fact, of a relativization of notions. For example, for young subjects an object cannot be both bigger than another and smaller than a third, because it cannot be both "big" and "little." Indeed, these terms remain affirmative and absolute—with the eventual possibility of a third class, that of "middle size"—and a characteristic *a* can then only be incompatible with *non-a*. Later, on the contrary, the attributes "big" and "little" become related, and then $\pm$ *a* becomes not only compatible with the $\mp$ *non-a,* but even equivalent to it.

This progressive overtaking [*dépassement*] of contradictions, which constitutes the formative process of differentiations as well as of coordinations, is fundamental when it comes to relations between operations and causality. To raise contradictions is, in effect, to construct a new operational structure. But, on the other hand, when these contradictions depend upon the interpretation of facts that are poorly noted or poorly explained, the coherence obtained concerns operations first applied, then attributed to objects. Consequently, the problem is to structure a content, and therefore to reach or to construct a new causal structure.

In the course of §§ 4–20, we have tried to show the positive contributions of operations to causality in their development, but also the constant reciprocal services that the second renders the first. In paragraphs II and III of this Conclusion, on the contrary, we noted how they oppose each other to the extent that they remain relatively undifferentiated. We now see that these latent conflicts due to undifferentiations are themselves sources of progress to the extent that contradictions constitute the motor of new coordinations. The whole of level IIB is particularly enlightening in this respect. On the one hand, it is at this level that the subjects complete "concrete" operations, which consequently permits a series of successes in their attributions to objects, and therefore in causality. For example, at about age 9 the construction of simple systems of coordinates goes hand in hand with successes in directions and, conversely, the differentiation of force and of movement favors that of stretchings and displacements, therefore the conservation of lengths, etc. On the other hand, the limitations of concrete operations entail systematic gaps in the solution of new problems in dynamics facing the subject, and even provoke contradictions to the extent that the subject does not succeed in dissociating by hypotheses the factors at work and proceeds only by serial correspondences of a global nature, resulting in the requirements of the overtaking [*dépassement*] that will lead to the construction of hypothetico-deductive or formal operations.

In general, the development of relationships between operations and causal explanations is therefore made up of a series of alternations between mutual supports (§§ 4–20) and fruitful oppositions, the sources of differentiations and coordinations. The final result is then twofold. On the one hand, each new problem that arises, whether from internal contradictions or from more extensive contradictions between the operations used and the structure of the objects, leads to the construction of new operational structures such as those in stage III following those in level IIB. On the other hand, and going even further, these differentiations and coordinations, whether operational or causal, eventually result in a progressive dissociation of levels: that of reality, therefore of contents and objects, and that of the operational forms of the subject, constructed in such a way that they can never again be contradicted by facts, which finally amounts to placing them on the level of hypothetico-deductive connections, and therefore direct and extratemporal connections between the possible and the necessary. That is what we must examine now.

The causal aspect of the action itself embraces its spatio-temporal dimensions, its speeds and its dynamism, whereas the logico-mathematical connections draw an abstraction from these physical conditions in order to retain only the form of coordinations. As for the coordinations, and even independent of the relationships of actions with objects, they still include as such, insofar as psychological processes are concerned, a certain dynamic aspect, a speed, a duration, etc. The retention only of their form, therefore, raises a similar problem. How can the form be dissociated from these ties with the general causality of the action? The logico-mathematical connections are essentially extratemporal and tie together only elements taken from succession and alteration that make them formal. The problem is, then, reduced to this: What steps in the thinking of the subject can be taken to go from a situation in which almost everything remains successive and causal to a situation permitting the selection of extemporaneous connections between forms that are stable or capable of being reestablished?

Two complementary processes lead to this result and therefore seem responsible for this progressive differentiation between the logico-mathematical and the causal. One is the effort to visualize total simultaneous representations of past, present, and future events, remaining successive on the level of perceptive observations. The other is the intervention of self-regulations, introducing in these systems a mobile equilibrium in such a way that the coordinations can be effected in both directions, direct and inverse (or reciprocal), and thus be transformed into reversible operations.[4]

But that is not the whole story, because if the process of equilibration, in the operational realm, not only makes it possible to link the states through reversible transformations, but also to confer a mobile stability on these transformations, that is not sufficient to ensure extemporaneity. Indeed, causal explanation proceeds in an analogous way by interpreting states of equilibrium by compensated transformations and by noncompensated transformations, starting with states of equilibrium. This is doubtless the result of an attribution to the objects of the play of operations, but this attribution is successful, and therefore the physical or causal forms and the operational forms of equilibrium have yet to be differentiated.

The difference exists and can be discerned starting with the

---

[4] Actually, the experiments of B. Inhelder, H. Sinclair, and M. Bovet on the development of operational structures by a method that facilitates the conscious realization of factors that observation shows to be important in the progress of this structuring, bring out the essential role of this passage from the successive to the simultaneous as well as regulations that result from it. It is in these experiments that we shall find the proof of what the observation of the development only suggests.

behavior in stage III, whereas the preceding considerations characterize the development leading from stage I to stage II. The physical notion of the virtual bears on the possibilities the compensations of which can be simultaneous, but the realizations of which are only consecutive, while all possibles remain simultaneous in the thinking process from the sole fact that they are conceived as possible. By nature, hypothetico-deductive reasoning goes directly from the possible to the necessary by connecting the possibles without the intermediary of reality. Besides, it is by this criterion that we can recognize the appearance of formal thought. As for its fruitfulness, all mathematics deals with the possible, and we do not need to dwell on it to see that this possible goes very far, and even infinitely in the proper sense of the term, beyond the frontiers of reality.

The fact that the possible and the real are opposites explains, in the final analysis, the multiple differences between operations and causality, which are so evident that there is no need to insist on them: absolute reversibility, conservation of initial data, complete deductibility, unlimited recurrence, intervention of the infinite, etc. To attribute operations to objects never means more than to find again in them what is compatible with the duration and with the complex relationships uniting the observable to the underlying structures. But since causality calls on structures for support and is not limited to the observable, an indefinite series of approximations can bring closer together causal and deductive systems.

(VII) Briefly, the differentiation between the operation and the causal depends on the progressive construction of its extemporaneous forms. But three questions remain: (1) Why this study of the extemporaneous? (2) How does it result in the constitution of "forms"? (3) What is their relationship with the forms of objects in causality between objects as opposed to that of the action itself?

(1) The tendency toward the extemporaneous by means of equilibration and reversibility depends on a vital need of thought and, from its roots, of the organism itself, which is to escape from the contradictions inherent in the successive events and, in time, to oppose some stability to the πάντασεῖ (*pantasie*) of the real. Starting with the most elementary regulations tending to compen-

sate for the external perturbations up to the higher formal operations bearing only on the possible, there is a study of coherence
and stability, the constant process of which is to avoid time.

(2) That being so, and once we admit that action itself is
initially both causal and coordinating, the passage from the action
to the operation is made by a gradual elimination of the dynamic
and kinematic factors that include the intervention of duration.
What remains, then, is a whole set of realities that must be called
"forms" since they are no longer physical. Their nature can be
accurately defined, at the risk of the most serious misunderstand-
ings, only by determining in a systematic way in what respects they
are richer or poorer than the causal transformations to which
they correspond. We have observed in connection with almost
every variety of causality recapitulated in this synthesis that we are
in the presence of a striking correspondence between the causal
structures of the object and the operational structures of the
subject, without being able to say either that the second ones derive
forthwith from the first or that the "attributions" of the second
ones to the first means a simple subjective projection. When a
causal structure (CS) of the object corresponds to an operational
structure (OS) of the subject, there is a common source (FS) to
be found in the mechanism of the action itself, and very specially
in the component functions F that express the regular dependencies inherent in these mechanisms. If that is so, and without specifying the modes of simple or reflexive abstractions in question in
the passage from FS to CS to OS, it would be absurd to present the
"forms" OS as simple figures or static elements, because they are
deprived of causal dynamism. These OS forms are operational
transformations comparable to causal transformations; that is, they
also are capable of indefinite "production," like their common
source FS, but they consist of formal constructions and not of
material effects. In this case, they certainly remain from one point
of view poorer than the CS, since everything dependent on time
is eliminated, time being the specific mark of the causality CS.
But they are otherwise enriched to the same degree, since the
elimination of the temporal, kinematics, and dynamics is *ipso facto*
an opening on the infinite world of possibles. As for their relationships with their own contents, in the case of applied or even at-

tributed operations, they enrich them not only by new relationships and by stability, but also by introducing in them this specific characteristic of all deductibility, which is necessity.

(3) If we now leave the relationships between these forms and the causality of objects and not just of the action, two remarks are in order. The first is that we cannot consider even the most general of these forms, namely, those of logic, as the residue of properties common to all the objects once the kinematic and dynamic factors are removed. The conception of logic as a "physics of any object whatever," held by H. Spencer and, in part, by Gonseth, forgets the transforming or productive character of operations, parallel and not inferior to that of causality, and the formula preserves only a truth modified into a "system of actions on any object whatever." In the second place, to the degree that there is correspondence between the causal transformations of objects and the operational transformations of the subject, it means neither that the latter are derived from the former, by simple elimination of dynamics in the relationships discovered through physical experiment, nor the converse, by simple projection of operations in the real. This correspondence is due to the fact that the action itself is both dependent on the physical laws of the object in general and also on the source of the operations of the subject. But in order for the subject to find again his operations in the real, a long development is necessary and a long series of "attributions" necessitating concurrently a gradual refinement of the physical experiment and a progressive construction of the operational instruments that make it possible. The problem, then, is one of relationships between the two types of abstractions that these two kinds of activities presuppose.

(VIII) Two fundamental data dominate the problems of physical knowledge and consequently the relationships between the operations of the subject and the causality of objects. The first was furnished by many previous studies, and we shall not dwell on it. It is that the reading of an experiment requires the use of instruments of assimilation to make this reading possible; in other words, it presumes the utilization of operational structures. For example, to judge that a quantity of liquid is conserved in the course of a transfer implies at least elementary means of quantification, a certain transitivity, if we wish to control the quantities in A and B, which have different shapes, by means of a container C similar to one or the other, etc. Consequently, a "simple" or physical abtraction, which naturally draws its information from the object, already presupposes connections made by the subject: "This stone is white" thus includes classes, a predictive relationship, etc., even independent of the language.

A second essential datum: Causal connections, while relying partially on information obtained through simple abstractions, inevitably go beyond the realm of the observable, even when it concerns the action itself, because then the movements of the subject, the resistance he succeeds in overcoming, etc., are for him observables that, like the others, are objective. Starting with perceptive causality, we see nothing going from the agent A to the recipient B, but, in terms of movements observed, we sense, as already mentioned, that "something has gone by." Now, this is a reconstitution, here due to regulations alone and to perceptive pre-inferences, but already comparable to deductive reconstitutions due to intelligence itself when it comes to transmissions at more complex levels. Indeed, we never observe anything other than displacements or qualitative changes, as well as speeds, but they are only the external manifestations of a causal relationship that must always be reconstructed by inferences and that thus inevitably goes beyond the frontier of the observable.

Let us now recall that we must distinguish what can be termed "reflexive abstractions" from "simple" or physical abstraction, which bears on observable characteristics only some of which are retained. In this case the information is no longer drawn from objects, or from the action as an observable object, but from the subject's actions or operations as coordinations, the latter being capable of being reflected in the pure or refined state, or again at the time when new relationships were introduced in the object by these coordinations, as, for example, objects coordinated, classified, or numbered by the subject. For example, multiplication is abstracted from addition, as addition of additions, proportions from multiplicative relationships and distributivity from proportions (see §12), etc.

It is therefore evident that the construction of operations relies on processes increasingly richer in reflexive abstractions. But what happens to causality if, of necessity, it goes beyond the observable? What happens to the contributions that the study of causality can make to the formation of new operations? In short, what happens to the processes of "application" or of "attribution" of the operations to the objects?

These problems arise when we reach the level of spatial transformations, especially of functions, since at their source these functions express dependencies or connections peculiar to the *schèmes* of the action and since this action "applies," in the mathematical sense of the word, to objects. As such, the functions constitute, like the action, the common source of operations and of causality, since they express in the first place the schematism of the actions. This double nature is translated in the following manner. On the one hand, if $y = f(x)$, the variants of x and y can be known by simple abstraction, if it is a question of observables, provided by studying the objects or the actions in their perceptible unfolding. But the reading of these observables already presupposes an establishment of relationships stemming from the coordinating activity of the subject, from which comes the covariant, which adds a relationship to the variants alone. *A fortiori,* the same applies to the idea of dependence, or univocal application to the right, with its orientation. In these relational elements, therefore, some reflexive abstraction, however minimal it may be, intervenes, but a necessary amount as found in every structure applied to the real for the purpose of discovering some regularity. In the second place, the covariations and dependencies of x and y can be due to the preoperational manipulations of the subject, for example, by displacements of the elements of one collection into another, in which case the role of reflexive abstraction becomes superior and the function then includes its own explanation or reason. Now let us suppose that a functional dependency discovered in the real has the same form as a dependency linked to these activities of the subject. As a result, this dependency will have a tendency to go beyond simple legality and to acquire a degree of necessity through a process analogous to the "attribution" from which causality is derived.

Spatial operations reveal an analogous situation. On the one hand, they permit the subject to construct forms and to transform them according to entirely deductible structural laws, indicating the necessary roles of reflexive abstractions. On the other hand, the objects themselves have figurative forms and a spatial organization which, as we saw in §9, are linked to their dynamics in a way analogous to that of the geometric constructions dependent on the actions of the subject. These spatial properties of the object can, therefore, give rise to experimental readings through a play of "simple" or physical abstractions. But this reading presupposes operational instruments constructed by reflexive abstractions, synonymous with the structures or operational forms, of the geometry of the subject. In this case there is, therefore, as in that of the function, continuous collaboration between the two types of abstractions.

To return to causality, the situation is paradoxically all the clearer, from the point of view of modes of abstractions, because if the facts and the laws for which we seek explanation are found by simple abstractions, the causal connection as such always goes beyond the realm of the observable. Since it has to be deduced, it can only be deduced by means of operations, and the source of these can be looked for only in the play of reflexive abstractions. But two fundamental circumstances complicate this picture at the outset: the attribution of these operations to the real and, from the very fact that they are attributable to it, the collaboration of the objects with the constitution of operations to come or with the enrichment by new morphisms of structures already constituted.

The attribution of operations to objects would not raise any question if it were based only on faith or if it were a spontaneous projection of the subject acting on the objects and finding in them respondents, the nature of which is comparable to science. But an attribution, to be established, must be verified, and this verification presupposes again the experiment, necessary for the control of explanatory hypotheses such as those that result in laws. This return to the experiment then requires a play of simple abstractions like those at the outset, but this time guided by a limited system of attributable operations. We therefore see which alternation between the two kinds of abstractions implies the attribution of operations to objects, because, as they are promoted to the rank of operators, they answer and correspond to the operations of the thinking subject while conserving their reality as external objects.

Now come two kinds of services that causality renders to operational structures, (1) by stimulating their formation through contents that lend themselves to such constructions and (2) by multiplying their morphisms at the time of attributions. Even though these contents are known through simple abstractions, they nonetheless require for their reading operational instruments due to reflexive abstraction. However, since this structuring of the contents at the levels of "applied" operations raises new problems that the previous operations cannot resolve, new operational constructions are then favored and thus the collaboration between the two kinds of abstractions becomes closer. *A fortiori,* the same is true at the time of the multiplication of the attributions.

In short, causality thus constitutes the principal partner in the shuttle game that constitutes the exchanges of the subject's operations with the real, and this is why it is difficult, in each particular causal explanation, to tell where the deductive contributions of the subject begin and where those that result from the kind of immanent, deductive construction that is causal production begin.

(IX) Nevertheless, by way of a conclusion, we must try to define these relationships more accurately and to determine what the preceding genetic data teach us about the nature of causality.

The first result of our analyses is that causality is not confused with legality, and that is just as true of our elementary stages as of the various levels of scientific knowledge. One of the first differences, as already mentioned, is that legality stems from evidence and bears on observable relationships, which, moreover, ordinarily interpret the regularities due to the interactions of the object and the manipulations of the experimenter. The causal connections, on the other hand, go beyond the frontiers of the observable. In the second place, legality achieves only general relationships, while causality includes necessary connections. Even in a function $y = f(x)$, in which the variations of y are supposed to depend objectively on those of x, this dependency constitutes only an established fact, not including any intrinsic necessity, as long as it is not accompanied by a beginning of causal attribution. In fact, in the third place, a law, even a general one, can stay isolated, while its causal explanation includes several relationships coordinated into a system and this system alone is the source of necessity. For example, in R49 the subject discovers, long before understanding the reason for it, that two weights pulling on strings separated from each other by a 30° to 60° angle have a resultant inferior to that of the same weights when the strings are closer together. However, this law, the truth of which is at first noted only in terms of a simple general fact, becomes necessary only once it is inserted in a system coordinating intensities and directions and especially implying the consequence that two equal and opposing forces cancel each other.

In the fourth place, legality includes only operations applied to objects, while, by virtue of its triple character of going beyond the observable, of reaching necessity, and of constituting systems, causality requires, in addition, an attribution of the same operations—but with also the transformations or compositions that they include—to the objects themselves. This hypothesis being at the core of our interpretation, it is wise to subject it to a retroactive examination in the light of the facts described in §§4–20. It is evident that legality implies the use of operations, and let us review it once more. From the reading of the facts until their inductive generalization, the subject needs to relate, classify, and quantify, without which every registering and every assimilation would be impossible. On the other hand, it is equally clear that, from the point of view of the subject himself, this logico-mathematical frame, which in reality he adds or "applies" to objects, seems to him to be a part of the objects, in such a way that, as far as the subject is aware, there exists no difference between applied and attributed operations. For the young child the words themselves seem at first to be a part of things. At all levels that will be all the more true of relationships, numbers, quantities, etc., and, finally, of every law conceived as the expression itself of reality. In this respect, the subject is not wrong, as long as we do not go beyond the phenomenon or the observable. For the observer, however, they are only the product of an interaction between the "things" and the instruments of assimilation of the subject, in such a way that, to reach the objects effectively, we must take another step and look for the underlying causal connections in the observables that tie them together. Then, but only then, begins the conquest of an objective universe, that is, where the objects exist and act as operators, therefore where the operations can be this time legitimately, although very partially, according to our language, "attributed" to the object.

Except for rare or marginal situations (problems that are too new, etc.), we do not find here two chronologically distinct phases, but simply two periods in the development of all physical knowledge, because the subject rarely stops at pure legality and, while waiting for the correct interpretations, is not deprived of approximate explanations, as we have consistently seen. It is even probable that, from the outset, it is the search for causality that functionally gives rise to the constitution of laws as a result of a condition prior to the determination of causes.

In addition, and without a sufficient justification of the abused expression "causal laws," we must recognize that at the very core of legality we often find a hint of causality, which is natural since, between an apparently simple relationship and a so-called structure, many intermediaries are conceivable because of combined differentiations and coordinations. For example, in R33 we see a slow perfecting of the laws of impact. A ball struck on its side at first goes in a straight line, then obliquely, and finally along a rectilinear path starting from the point of impact and going through its center, while the active ball goes almost at a right angle. In this case we are not far from a structure basically made up of actions and reactions as well as of compositions of vectoral directions, in other words, of a coherent causal system, and the groundwork has been laid by legitimate approximations. Likewise, a law of conservation leads sooner or later to a structure approaching a group, etc.

We now come to the second general result of our studies, namely, the interpretation of causality as operational structures attributed to the object. One of the first evidences is that these "attributed" operations are not simply added on top of those that were "applied" in the constitution of legality. They are the same operations, at least at the outset, even though they might be completed by others of the same kind, and what is new is only the deductive link, and therefore the coordinations uniting them from then on. Indeed, a deductive link is necessary, going beyond the observable and constituting a system, and therefore presenting the three differential characteristics previously noted. The nature of causality thus always includes a system of transformations that cannot be reduced to a simple relationship of cause and effect presupposed by common sense. Even in cases where such a relationship seems to exist, as in the example of a push, there intervenes in reality an elementary structure, that is, compensations between losses and gains, composition of transformations and conservations, etc., not to mention directions—in other words, a deductive system. But then why does this deductivity entail an attribution of the structure in addition to a simple application? It would be easy, and it is even a frequent positivist or conventionalistic thesis, to conceive the model so constructed as a simple subjective instrument satisfying the mind but not corresponding as such to the nature of things, since neither this nature nor these things are indispensable to a coherent conventionalism.

The second evidence that seemed to emerge is, on the contrary, that the transformations included in a system or deductive model connecting together the operations until then applied only to objects, having meaning, if confirmed by the experiment and, therefore, in conformity with legality thus enlarged, only in the hypothesis in which these objects "exist" and in which, consequently, the transformations mentioned express more or less adequately their real actions.

The fact is all the more striking since the deductive system on which the causal explanation is based does not consist of a simple arrangement of laws or of their contents, fitting into each other [*emboîtement*] by a syllogistic chain of reasoning [*enchaînment*] of the type "water always flows because it is light," going into "light things are not held back by themselves," etc., as with the young subjects of R32. It really consists of a composition of applied operations themselves arrived at by means of general procedures of coordination and of operational transformations, that is, transitivity, multiplicativity, reciprocity, etc. It is, indeed, these general forms of operational organization that constitute structures, to the extent that its internal compositions close in on themselves when necessary. It is precisely in this case that the coordination of applied operations could not appear as a simple necessity relative to the subject and seems to base the legal relationships on an external and ontic substratum, which is the characteristic of causality leading to the "attribution" of the structure to reality.

The reason for this is that one phenomenon transformed into another ends up in more than a conjunction of two phenomena and that the unobservable connection thus constructed acquires a power of objectivation to the degree that it is tied to a structure. When an action of the subject, at first free and isolated, is linked to others at the core of an operational structure, the structure also acquires a kind of "intrinsic" objectivation which requires no foundation or externalization. On the other hand, when an operation applied to the object, with experimental success making this application legitimate, is coordinated with another also applied in a valid way, then the structure that they will constitute requires, as a result of these successful applications, an objectivation of an extrinsic nature. Finally, since the structure transcends the observable, it can, by virtue of this objectivation, constitute objects going beyond the phenomena, the causal actions of which correspond to the transformations of the system. Such seem to be the reasons for the numerous "attributions" of the operational structures previously described.

For example, for the transmissions of movements in R2, the laws founded on the observable are based only on the regularity, discussed by Hume, of the launching of one ball hit by another, and, in the case of a row of contiguous intermediaries, of the launching of the last marble untouched by the active marble. Starting with the most precocious levels, the first of these two regularities is accompanied, we have seen, by a causal impression that already rests on an elementary "structure," that is, loss of the movement of the active marble and gain of the passive one, therefore a composite of transformation and conservation sufficient to explain the transmission in its "external" form but not taking into account the "how." With the launching of the last marble in a row, this model is simply generalized, which takes the "how" even less into account. The nature of the operational transformation constituted by transitivity is, on the contrary, to link together the diverse observations of laws with their corresponding but only local beginnings of causality (one impact + one impact + etc.), which then permits an attribution to objects in the form of the transmission of a "current" that goes through them. For a set of local structures each of which already goes beyond a pure system of legality as far as structure is concerned, and which consequently includes a beginning of attributions, there is therefore substituted a structure of the whole, the degree of attribution of which is appreciably "greater." Likewise, in the many observable situations of action and reaction, legality is based only on regularities in the form of slow-downs or returns; therefore the corresponding beginnings of causality can consist only of models of braking or of rebounding through deviations of impetus, etc. On the contrary, the total structure furnished by the coordination of inversions and reciprocities permits the general attribution to the objects of a force of reaction in response to the actions, etc.

Starting with our modest facts relative to the psychogenesis of causality, we are struck by the fact that we are in the presence of an evolution that, in certain aspects, presents an analogy to that of contemporary physics.[5] Nineteenth-century physics consisted essentially of measuring and developing laws that require no logico-mathematical instruments other than operations "applied" to objects. No doubt, the tendencies toward "attribution" were already common, but on the other hand, generally contested—for example, the atomistic hypotheses, due to the operational structures of splitting, or the belief in the existence of forces in the expression $a = f/m$ or again $m = f/a$ (Euler) instead of the simple relationships $f = ma$. On the other hand, contemporary physics is oriented toward the study of structures that will be expressed in the form of models capable of becoming axioms, tying together laws by a necessary deduction and establishing then the possibility of a series of attributions based on reason. In this case, what ensures the legitimacy of these transformations, attributed to objects, is the need for them to be operational as, for example, when a law of conservation is integrated in a group that requires its intervention. Of course, the axioms of such models are suggested by the facts. The deductions derived from them must be controlled by facts,

[5] Except at the level of scientific thought, the "application" and the "attribution" of operations are more differentiated, and therefore often occur with time lags between them.

but the remarkable character of such a theoretical physics is that, to the extent that it has taken an additional step in the direction of the logico-mathematical construction, the necessary transformations thus attained on the level of the possible and of the abstract structures can give rise to more advanced and better-justified "attributions." This is the surprising equivalence between the operational coordinations of the subject and the causal connections of the objects, certain preliminary steps of which we have studied.

(X) On the whole, operations constitute, so to speak, a causality applicable to extratemporal forms and physical causality, a system of operations brought about by the material objects. The reason for these correspondences is clearly that the source of operations is to be found in regulations of the organism and that the organism is a physical object subject to causality like all other objects. But then why does the subject not know, through the medium of his organism, the totality of causes and effects that are centered in him, or at least the totality of those that rule his interactions with the environment? It is because knowledge is not a reflection but an activity, and because our knowledge of causality is something other than causality and proceeds by various laborious approximations. These begin only with actions, that is, with higher forms of the interactions between the organism and the objects external to it. But if the action undergoes all the causal processes of the organism and the environment, it becomes aware of these processes only to the extent that it controls them actively. This is the reason for the original primacy of the mechanical causality linked to well-controlled manual actions, etc., and the considerable delay in acquiring the concepts of heat and light.

With this in mind, if the cognitive structuring thus begins at the periphery of the organism by means of actions and with beginnings of awareness depending on the extent of their controls, we then understand the close solidarity of the progress, or of its delay, in the double direction of the conquest of reality with causality, and of the development of controls and operations, which are the internal coordinations of the subject. We understand in particular that for every progress of these endogenous structures, proceeding by reflexive abstractions, there is a corresponding refinement of the experiment and of physical or simple abstractions, and conversely, there is a complementary solidarity between those two modes of abstraction that, in the end, is only the expression of two inter-dependent movements, although going in opposite directions, of externalization in the grasping of reality and of internalization in the construction of the instruments of assimilation.

PART TWO

Physico-Geometric Explanations and Analysis

by R. Garcia and J. Piaget

The ambition of genetic epistemology has always been to link the problems that arise at the most elementary levels of knowledge to those raised by the theory of scientific thought itself. In fact, problems such as those of the formation of a number, the role of correspondences or "applications" of relationships between the notions of time and velocity, the relationships between the permanence of objects and spatio-temporal localization, etc., have always not only permitted but forced us to attempt such coordinations, because it seems almost evident that the actual outcomes of such concepts or structures are not entirely independent of their mode of construction, starting with their prescientific roots.

Concerning the psychogenesis of causal explanations, two problems in particular, which seem to be found at all stages in the development of physics and the terms of which have been renewed by a number of works on theoretical physics, have come up recently. The first is that of relationships between the geometric operations of the subject and the space of objects, insofar as the former stem from logico-mathematical structures and the latter from physical experience. The second concerns the relationships between this physical space and dynamics. The problem is to determine to what point the geometry of objects remains necessarily solidary with a dynamic and not only kinematic model, or whether it becomes independent of that model and, as some contemporaries think, can even end in a return to the Cartesian postulate of a total reduction of phenomena to "figures" and "movements."

In this second part we would like to present a discussion of these two problems by combining the resources of genetic epistemology and epistemological analysis inherent in theoretical physics. This essay, therefore, constitutes an attempt at interdisciplinary research.

I. The Given of Genetic Epistemology

1. Geometric Operations and Space of Objects

To return to the most elementary forms of knowing, let us first remember that we note at all levels the essential distinction between physical knowledge, in the broad sense of the word, and the logico-mathematical connections, as admitted by so many authors, including contemporary positivists. However, this opposition does not end up with that of synthetic and analytical judgments, as Quine has proved and as we have verified by showing the existence of numerous genetic intermediaries among them,[1] neither could it be brought back to the distinction between language and experience. Indeed, on the one hand, starting with the level of sensori-motor *schèmes* prior to language, we find relationships of order, nestings [*emboîtements*], correspondences, etc., which already stem from logico-mathematical structures. On the other hand, along with the physical experience, which draws its information from the properties of the object, we can speak of a logico-mathematical experience when the information is abstracted from the actions or operations performed by the subject on the objects or from properties, order, classes, sums, etc., that these actions

[1] Vol. IV of the *Etudes*.

temporarily introduce in the objects. With such a perspective, we can therefore admit that physical knowledge tries to reach the object by removing it from the orbit of the subject, while the logico-mathematical connections express at the outset the general coordinations of the action, including those that are found again in every language capable of form and finally in every operational structure.

With this understanding, the nature of spaces, in the usual meaning of the word, is the ability to give rise both to operational constructions of a deductive nature, as is the case in mathematical spaces, and to physical findings stemming from experiments bearing on the objects. Beginning with the most elementary and even sensori-motor levels, we can distinguish these two poles: the construction of the practical group of displacements between 12 and 18 months thus includes inferential mechanisms, while the multiple perceptions relative to the forms and dimensions of the objects are certainly derived from data inherent in the physical experience.

When we come to the operational and deductive aspects of space, it is particularly striking to note the close parallelism that genetically links the formation of spatial with logico-arithmetic operations, even though the spatial operations bear on the continuum and on relationships of neighborhoods, while the logico-arithmetic ones group discrete objects according to their qualitative resemblances and differences. The fitting together [*emboîtement*] of the parts of a continuum, the order of positions, the measure through synthesis of these separations and of the orderly displacement of the unit, the coordinates, etc., are thus constructed in correspondence, but not by simple filiation, with the inclusions of classes, seriations, number through the synthesis of nestings [*emboîtements*], and of order, the multiplicative structures, that is, Cartesian products, serial multiplications, etc., with two or three logical dimensions, etc.

As for the empirical observations pertaining to physical space, it is to be carefully noted that, if they clearly find certain properties of the objects, that is, certain data existing independent of the activities of the subject, they reach them only through the intermediary of the preceding operations, or of the preoperations that herald them, and which are then "applied" to these objects. Starting with the perception of geometric "good forms," such as a circle or a square, we encounter schematizations in the double meaning of Gonseth's "schéma" of simplification and *"schèmes* of assimilation,"* on the role of which one of us has always insisted. For example, if we try to measure the resistance of a good perceptive form—for example, by adding "pennures" to the upper and lower sides of a square, as in Müller-Lyer's illusion, which tends to make them perceptibly unequal—we note that this resistance varies according to the operational level of the subject, etc. The conservation of lengths in cases of displacement (which amounts, for instance, to admitting that the shape of a ruler does not change when it is moved a few centimeters) is recognized by the subject at about age 9, only if he succeeds in evaluating these lengths metrically (interval between the extremities) and thus in correcting the initial ordinal estimation, that is, the order of the points of arrival or the consideration of protrusions [*dépassements*] in the direction of the movement, from which comes the criterion "longer = going farther." The horizontality of the level of water is admitted only by using interfigural references, but up to age 9 this surface is predicted only in terms of intrafigural reference, and therefore in terms of the shape of the receptacle that is tipped, etc.

In short, there exists from the outset an operational space and spatial properties inherent in objects, but the former is not simply derived from the latter nor the opposite, and the latter can be reached only through the intermediary of the former. However, the spatial operations we have been talking about up to now are still, in this last case, only operations "applied" to the object, that is, used by the subject himself in his readings of the experiment, as instruments of registration or assimilation for the purpose of his own findings but without reference to the causality of objects.

A second problem is thus immediately raised: Of what does this physical space or space of objects consist? It is by nature operational, or is its structure different and more or less foreign to that of the operations used by the subject in order to reach it? In the case of the horizontality of the level of water, for example, it is clear, for the subject capable of perceiving it, that it is the water itself that gives to its surface a level and horizontal form; it is not the experimenter, even though he tips the jar in various positions.

How does the water do it, as interpreted by the subject? As evidenced by the study of the explanation of causality, it is the water, as an object independent of the subject, that becomes a spatial operator, since it gives itself a form and constantly reconstitutes itself despite changes in orientation of the receptacle. In this case we shall speak of operations "attributed to the object" and no longer only "applied" by the subject as instruments necessary for reading the experiment.

The multiple studies on causality have demonstrated that it amounts exactly to sets of operations attributed to objects—in other words, to operational structures considered as inherent in the "actions" of objects in their multiple interactions. The problem is then to establish the role of physical space or of spatial operations attributed to objects at the core of these causal structures.

2. *The Space of Objects and Physical Causality*

One of the first evident differences between the operational space of the subject and the physical space of the objects is that physical space is spatio-temporal, while the spatial operations of the subject are extra-temporal. Thus an operational displacement is only a change in position, with six parameters when it is measured in meters, while a real or physical movement takes time, and therefore includes speed. Even the static forms of solids are a function of duration, since they are conserved for a long or short time depending on the degree of nondeformability of the objects they characterize. At all levels of development, the geometry of the objects is therefore solidary with kinematics. This raises no psychogenetic problem given the very early understanding of the notion of speed at first founded on the ordinal intuition of overtaking [*dépassement*], like lengths themselves, long before it is considered as a relationship, etc. The only question to be raised from the point of view of spatio-temporal structures is the initial heterogeneity of full and empty spaces. When, for example, no solid is placed between two objects A and B, the distance AB is, until about age 7 to 8, judged to be greater than when a wall is placed between A and B.

In this case the thickness of the wall is of another spatial nature and is therefore to be deducted, whereas if the wall has holes, the distance remains the same. The homogenization of the filled lengths and the empty distances thus raises a problem whose solution is probably linked to the constitution of systems of references, therefore to interfigural relationships. But since the latter depend equally on the progress of causal interaction, as we shall see, this question becomes part of all those that have yet to be proposed.

Indeed, if the physical space is solidary with kinematics, psychogenetic analysis likewise shows that, at all levels of development, it is closely linked with interpretations of dynamics. This is understood from the beginning for the general reason that, until age 9, force cannot be dissociated from movement, not only because no force is conceivable except in movement ("impetus" [*élan*], etc.), and this until about age 11 to 12, but because until age 7 to 8 inclusive, every movement encompasses a force in the form of an "internal motor," as Aristotle claimed, even if the necessity for an additional "external motor" is recognized. The primitive notion seems to be one of "action" in the sense of *fte* or of *mve,* which makes any kinematics consonant with dynamics. The undifferentiation of movement and force is periodically found in the history of physics, and we still come across traces of it in bad manuals in connection with centrifugal "force," which gave rise to stern comments by Hertz.

The first example of this solidarity between physical space and dynamics is that of the conservation of lengths, already cited from the point of view of operations "applied" by the subject to the finding of facts, but which now must be taken up again in the perspective of operations "attributed" to the object. Indeed, from this second point of view, the movement of a ruler A which we displace in relation to another ruler $B,$ after the subject has verified the congruence $A = B$ by placing one ruler on top of the other, stems from a spatial operator; for the child up to about age 9, the problem is to know which operator. If the movement can be reduced to a simple operator of displacement when the length of the object is recognized as invariant, it can likewise consist of an operator of lengthening or stretching as if the ruler were elastic. In fact, observation shows, with dynamics intervening at this point, that these two operators remain undifferentiated for a long time, for reasons at once dynamic (nature of the movement transmitted as *fte*) and geometric (lack of references). On the one hand, the ruler is supposed to lengthen and not just move. The subject will thus flatly state that the extension of *A* in relation to *B* is greater than the reciprocal extension, *B* to *A,* even though he can see it at the other end. On the other hand, when we have him mark the lengthening of an elastic, or that of three springs placed end to end after he has verified that they have been stretched equally, when hung parallel to each other and provided with the same weights, this lengthening is conceived as a simple displacement of the ends pulled, with a complete absence of distributivity or of homogeneous dilation even in the case of the three springs. There is therefore undifferentiation between the additive displacements and the multiplicative lengthenings. The reason is that the passive mobile still includes an "internal motor." When, on the contrary, about age 9 to 10, the notions of movement and force are sufficiently differentiated, the passive mobile is simply subjected to the effects of an active force, and its movements are then distinguished according to the two classes, displacements and lengthenings, in comparison with starting points, fixed in the case of the elastic or of the springs held in place, variable in the case of the ruler, and with arrival points as well as in reference to an external system. At the same time, we note that these relationships, which are only geometric with internal or external references that could have appeared accessible independently of any dynamics, are, in fact, constructed only when the forces and movements are sufficiently differentiated.

This solidarity of spatial references and dynamics, already clear but surprising in a problem as simple as the conservation of lengths, is even more evident in the case of natural coordinates, vertical and horizontal. It is thus that the horizontality of the surface of water is anticipated when the container is tipped is only anticipated, or even observed (otherwise the reading as such remains inexact) at the level when it is understood causally. Until about age 9, water is "light" and spreads anywhere. When it becomes "heavy" it tends to go toward the bottom and, in the case of a level momentarily tipped, the upper layers tend to slide on the lower ones up to a point of equalization at a median horizontal level. Likewise, in the case of verticality when one lets go a tipped stick, until about age 9 it is supposed to fall in the direction of its leaning and not vertically, while at the level where natural co-ordinates are worked out, its fall is vertical whatever its original orientation. Here again, this dynamic progress in the interpretation of the role of weight necessarily interferes with the construction of special references, just as in the case of water. In this respect let us recall that for young subjects more force is required to hold in place a cart on an inclined plane than to make it go up because the cart has a tendency to go down when it is immobile, and this tendency disappears when it is pulled up because of the very fact that it is pulled up. Starting with age 8 to 9 this tendency becomes general, and it is the late mastery of the dynamics of descent or fall that result in the success of the preceding tests.

Another field in which spatial factors constantly interact with dynamics is that of directions. When young subjects push a little board with a pencil at a point other than opposite the center, they do not expect to see it turn but think that they are giving a move-ment "straight" ahead. Likewise, when one ball hits another on its side, the passive ball is supposed to start out along the extension of the path of the active one, etc. In tests of this kind, the coordina-tion of translations and rotations or the deviations of the two balls, when the impact is not given in full force, are understood only when the role of resistance is admitted and the geometrization ad-vances only in proportion with the progressive solution of the problems of dynamics. Likewise, the law of the equality of angles of incidence and reflection, in the case of impact against a recti-linear wall, is predicted only insofar as the subject glimpses models of the action and reaction type.

In short, physical space clearly acquires an operational structure because of the geometric operations of the subject himself, since he could not attribute to the objects spatial operations other than those mastered in his own actions. But that does not mean that this geometrization is a one-way development from the subject to objects. On the contrary, it is the extent to which the problems of dy-namics require new constructs that the constructs are built little by little in such a way that, in the final analysis, the total space of the

objects can be deduced from their dynamics. Indeed, dynamics includes spatial operations. As we have seen, the reading as such
of the relationships in question already presupposes applied operations. However, when it is a question of going from application
to attribution, the space of objects cannot be dissociated from
other components, and it is within the causal interpretations, in the
totality of each particular explicative system, that geometrization
is achieved. It is therefore possible to conclude that however much
the geometric operations of the subject and the spatial operators
ascribed to objects correspond to each other, the first remain more
linked to logico-arithmetic operations while the second acquire a
constantly dynamic meaning.

3. *Problems of Analysis or Reciprocal Assimilation*

Even in the group aged 11 or 12 to 15, at which time propositional or formal operations, combinatory and quarternions, are
developed, the causal explanations that the child may arrive at are
not pursued far enough to enable us to determine with profitable
results whether they reveal a progressive reduction of mechanics to
geometry or whether they point to a reciprocal assimilation between two sets of factors. Certainly, their increasingly closer
union, particularly in the case of vectoral compositions (age 11 to
12), when the subject understands the modification of resultants in
cases of invariable intensities and variable directions or the reverse, seems to reveal a progressive integration in both directions.
On the other hand, the constant solidarity that we have mentioned
between physical space and dynamics seems to suggest that, if it is
to be reckoned with from its beginning, it must constitute a more
or less constant characteristic of this space of objects.

Therefore, we shall now proceed to a comparison with the history of science. The aim of the present section is to pose certain
problems, the rest of this essay being given to their solution. To
this end we shall find an analysis of the different stands taken by

physics from the seventeenth century to the present. After Descartes had unsuccessfully dreamed of a physics reduced entirely to geometry (figures and movements), that geometry bearing on an "extension" parallel to "thought" and therefore to algebra, combining both in analytic geometry, Newton reintroduced dynamism, but by conceiving space with time as a container and dynamics as a content, the relationships between the two being conceived as those of a necessary adjustment but without interaction as such.

With the theory of relativity, a force of attraction at a distance is dispensed with, and gravity can be reduced to a system of inertial movements whose trajectories follow the curves of a Riemannian space. At first glance, we find in this an integral geometrization, therefore a return to a Cartesian ideal with a total reduction of dynamics to space-time, which is how it was interpreted by various authors, including Meyerson and sometimes H. Weyl. But Einstein himself admitted a really reciprocal assimilation. If heavy bodies follow the curvatures of space, these curvatures are in fact provoked by masses, in such a way that there is still a dynamics and a space or a space-time but maintaining between them relationships of solidarity unknown to Newton. Indeed, while Newton limited himself to the relationships of container to content, with Einstein these become interdependent, such an interaction having been meticulously analyzed by Brunschvicg.

On the other hand, to a number of contemporaries (see §§ 9 and 10) all mass and every dynamic process are reduced to forms or to geometric transformations in such a way that no body or any physical event is any longer to be situated *in* space. They are themselves parts *of* space, the analysis dreamed of by Descartes thus appearing to become an effective reality.

But if we compare this ultimate phase of thinking in physics to its origin, two groups of problems inevitably arise. It is on their solutions that the epistemological interpretation, idealistic or realistic, of these works, and finally the survival or elimination of dynamism, will depend.

(1) The first set of questions deals with the nature of the operations used. Are we dealing with operations belonging only to the geometry of the subject and permitting him to construct models independent of a convergence of details with reality existing inde-

pendent of us? Or are we dealing with operations "attributed to objects," even if these objects no longer have any connection with what our perceptions, subjective but customary, ordinarily associate with this term and remain "objective" only from a cognitive point of view that is broadened and intellectually refined?

(a) Once we remember that the spatial operations of the subject are extemporaneous, a preliminary subproblem consists in asking ourselves what is implied by the spatio-temporal character of the physical spaces used by the theories in question. It is not sufficient to answer that, mathematically, time is simply made up of a fourth dimension. The question is to know whether the irreversibility peculiar to this dimension, as opposed to the other three, already furnishes some indication of the "applied" or "attributed" character of the operations that use it. If we say that an electron is expelled by a photon or that a photon disappears and transfers its energy hv—or is identical to it but then changes form—wouldn't we be attributing these operations to the events as such even if we were to translate these events into pure geometric operation? Indeed, if the physicist-subject can, because of his own operations, easily return to the period of time preceding the expulsion of the electron or the destruction of the photon, the operations used to interpret the process cannot be reversed, because we are dealing with the events themselves in their irreversibility, and the group *PCT* which thought it could reverse them was definitely not attributable to reality. The spatio-temporal, and not just the spatial, character is therefore one of the first indications of the "attributed" character of the operations in question, since time is related to events and the latter imply a causality.

(b) The second subproblem consists of asking ourselves what a physical object is epistemologically, and whether this notion disappears in the case of integral geometrization. The nature of an object of thought or a logico-mathematical object is such that the operations of the subject can transform it at will. A rhombus, for example, can be displaced, changed in size, stretched by refined transformations, projected, etc., or changed into an entirely different figure with the sole proviso of setting up its own coherent rules of transformations. The latter are therefore unlimited, provided that they are not contradictory, and the problem is not to make them possible, but only to choose the most interesting ones from among the infinite number of possibilities. A physical object, on the contrary, obeys laws that the subject cannot change and that he can transform only within the framework fixed by these laws. If such is the case, thinking of it as reducible to spatio-temporal elements does not change its nature as an object, even if it takes the forms of a group of waves or of a corpuscle and even if we think of the latter as some part of space by putting aside all that our tactilo-kinesthetic and visual perceptions attach to the different "bodies" that on our level we commonly call "objects."

(c) In the third place, an essential difference contrasts the operations of the subject with those that are attributed to objects so conceived. Although the operations of the subject cannot be contradicted by experience, the validity of the operations of objects is subordinated to its control. It is clear that if the spatialization of objects in physics facilitates the construction of deductive models, in no way can they be exempt from confirmation by the experimental facts themselves. There is therefore a decisive reason for considering the operations in question as being attributed to objects.

On the whole, it seems evident that the spatio-temporal or kinematic entities to which the new theories try to reduce physics are nevertheless conceived as independent of the subject. That means that the operations characterizing their structures are attributed to them and are not subjective in the sense of idealism. Since such an attribution appears to constitute the most general characteristic of causal explanation, the problem is thus to try to establish whether this causality is reduced to a kinematic analysis or whether it includes some dynamism.

(II) The second group of problems we have to consider must therefore focus on the meaning of this causality and on how much eventual dynamism causality will allow. In general, the analogies between operational compositions and causality amount to this: that both include a synthesis of transformations, taking into account the novelty of the results, and of conservation ensuring the connection between the conditions at the time of departure and arrival. On the other hand, the difference is that the operational compositions are due to the activity of the subject, while causality is the work of objects conceived as operators. Now, in the usual causal models, in which masses, actions, forces, and energies intervene, the parallelism between causality and operations is approximated only to the precise degree that this dynamism remains foreign to nontemporal structures. In the case of a complete geometrization of reality, the isomorphism between the objects and the operations of the subject tends, on the contrary, to become complete. Must we then conclude from it an elimination of dynamism and of causality itself?

(a) The prime reason to doubt it is that, if physical reality is conceived as the locus of spatio-temporal transformations, there remains a rather fundamental difference between them and the geometric transformations due to the subject. As far as the latter are concerned, the power is, as we have just seen, in the hands of the subject himself. To say that the subject constitutes only a locus or a stage and that the operations play the game by themselves does nothing to change the situation, because each operation is an act and it is their totality, effective or virtual, that constitutes the subject. When, on the contrary, a series of reactions occurs within a system, it is not by considering each element as a spatio-temporal figure, therefore a "form," that we escape the evidence of an interaction between such "forms." Indeed, if these "forms" are not those constructed by the subject, therefore if they constitute objects independent of us, it is clear that these "forms" act on each other, transform each other, and therefore exercise a power on each other. Now, whereas the power of logico-mathematical operations remains nontemporal, a spatio-temporal power implies a succession in time, and therefore cannot be prevented from being assimilated with a causal relationship, since there is both an action of one "object" on another as long as these objects, though geometric, do not depend on us and a chain reaction as long as they also possess [*enchâinement*] kinematics.

(b) If this is so, we are led to presuppose the existence of dynamics, however refined it may be in relation to habitual intuitions. In everyday language, there exist bodies and movements, with dynamics intervening when any of them changes. To geometrize all that, bodies become "forms," and it is to them that movements are attached. But since each of these forms preserves the power to modify others as well as its own movements, it is this "power" that plays a dynamic role. This role is indispensable, since it cannot be distinguished from the reality of objective transformations, the existence of which cannot be denied. Space-time is then only the coordination of such interactions—in other words, the "field" characterized by the connection between these events (see the end of § 10).

(c) Indeed, the principal interest of this dynamics is that it stays immanent in the operators in question. Now, since the latter are isomorphic (because they are geometric) to the operations of the subject, their dynamism, although physical by nature, can escape analysis to the extent that we forget that the "forms" in question are in fact objects, because they are autonomous and not organized by us. On the other hand, insofar as we make explicit all the physical presuppositions of the system, such a geometrization not only includes nothing idealistic, but also appears as a logical outcome of this perpetual, reciprocal assimilation of spatial and dynamic structures, which takes shape beginning with the elementary stages in the development of causality. This assimilation has even become so complete that we can speak of it as a "dynamic geometrism," or as Garcia will state, of a "geometrodynamics" and not only of two successive periods of the doctrine.

II. Positions of Physicists

4. Analytical Trends of Thought in Mechanics

Ever since the physicists of the seventeenth century arrived at the theory of mechanics, which reached its peak with Newton, the problem of interpreting the basic concepts on which the theory rests has remained unsolved. The relationship between geometry and mechanics, that is, between physical space provided with certain geometric properties and matter, is the crux of the disagreements between the different interpretations.

Newton established the doctrine that became the "official" position of physics until the end of the nineteenth century. Space exists independent of the objects occupying it, and time exists independent of the objects and of the processes that go on. It is true that Newton geometrized physics, to the degree that the laws he formulated and the operations he defined reduced the solution of mechanical problems to the application of a method of computation. A. Koyré, in his *Etudes newtonnienes* (p. 29), considers that one of the most important characteristics of the Newtonian revolution is "the geometrization of space, that is, the substitution of space-dimension, homogeneous and abstract, of Euclidean geometry (however then considered as real) for the continuous whole, concrete and differentiated, of the 'loci' of preGalilean physics and astronomy." And he adds: "In fact, this characterization is almost equivalent to the mathematization (geometrization) of nature and consequently to the mathematization (geometrization) of science." However, his geometrization did not solve the problem, but presented it even more sharply. Space has its own geometry, which is Euclid's. The things that occupy this space have properties that can be expressed by numbers, for example, mass. These numbers are considered as values of arguments of functions, which are connected by means of principles or laws. The movement of bodies can, from that time on, be "explained" by the conduct of these functions. The geometric properties of the functions therefore correspond to the properties of movement. But the movement itself is determined by the properties of objects.

Before Newton's *Principia,* Descartes had already tried to reduce physics to mechanics, and mechanics to geometry. The sole property of matter retained by Descartes is extension, which is a geometric property: "Those who pretend to distinguish material substance from extension or from quantity, either have no idea of substance or else have a confused idea of an immaterial substance." Nevertheless, Descartes did not accept the existence of an independent physical space, that is, an empty space. There is an ambiguity that has never been resolved by the Cartesians: Extension is linked to bodies but is also identified with space. For that reason, Descartes rejected absolute space but, at the same time, treated space as a fundamental notion in his essay on the geometrization of mechanics.

Huyghens and Leibniz "contested" Newton's position with greater depth and coherence than the Cartesians. Absolute space and time were rejected. The geometric properties of physical space, as well as temporal relationships, were due to physical events.

Starting with this historic period we can speak, to a certain extent, of a dialectic game that goes through different steps, in which the concept that scientists have of motion oscillates between a subordination of geometry to the properties of matter and a determined emphasis on the geometric aspects. Huyghens, Leibniz, Riemann, Clifford, Mach, and Einstein are in the first group. Descartes, d'Alembert, Lagrange, Hamilton, Hertz, and a few of the contemporary proponents of relativity, such as Misner and Wheeler, are in the second. Of course, neither of these lists is exhaustive, nor is the distinction always very clear. Our intention is not to make an in-depth historical analysis, but rather to show two trends of thought, which constitute in our opinion two converging lines of progress. The Newtonian position remained, even after the major revision of its foundations dating to the end of the nineteenth century. Even so, Whitehead tried to return to a dualism, structured space-matter, within the relativistic context. In his book, *The Principle of Relativity,* he emphatically declares: "Inherent in my theory is the maintenance of the former division between physics and geometry. Physics is the science of contingent relationships of nature, and geometry expresses its uniform relatedness."

5. *Huyghens and Leibniz Against Newton*

Newton's mechanics is based on a theory of absolute motion. In the Introduction to the *Principia,* Newton gives definitions of absolute space and time. Space and time are characterized as entities that exist independent of objects and that furnish the measure of spatio-temporal events. Newtonian space must be considered as being at rest. When he introduces acceleration in his laws of motion, it is evident that he means acceleration in relation to space.

Nevertheless, it is important to emphasize that Newton's need to introduce an absolute space comes from dynamics and not from kinematics. The state of motion of a body is manifested by the occurrence of *forces*. In the famous polemic between Leibniz and Clarke, the latter, who evidently speaks as a representative of Newton, refers to centrifugal force as the last and irrefutable proof of an absolute motion. Curiously, the Introduction to the *Principia* contains an explicit declaration of the author according to which he "has not considered their principles as a physicist but simply as a geometrician."

Despite the enormous revolution brought about by the Newtonian concept of mechanics, the very foundations on which the new structure was built were "contested" from its origin. For our purpose, the two most important contestants—except for the Cartesians—were Huyghens and Leibniz.

According to Leibniz, only physical objects and their states are presupposed as "given," and it is on the basis of some of their relationships that we construct the order of time and space. Causality is the physical relationship that leads to order in time. If two physical states are in a cause-and-effect relationship, the cause is *defined* as the anterior state and the effect as the posterior state. "Time is the order of nonsimultaneous things." And "space is the order of coexistent things." According to Leibniz, there is no "absolute reality outside things."

Leibniz is a relativist in his concept of motion. Nevertheless, he admits that "in reality each body has a certain degree of motion or, if you wish, force," and from there he goes on to conclude that "there exists in nature something that geometry cannot determine." Except for extension, which is purely geometric, there is something that is more important and that determines motion: force. Motion thus acquires a metaphysical meaning: "Having tried to go deeper into the very principles of mechanics in order to account for the laws of nature, which experience revealed to us, I noticed that the consideration alone of an *extended mass* was not sufficient and that it was still necessary to use the notion of *force,* which is very intelligible although it belongs to metaphysics." Nevertheless, Leibniz rejected the Newtonian concept of gravity, which he found inexplicable. In his letter to Huyghens dated October, 1690, he declares: "After having carefully considered Mr. Newton's book which I saw in Rome for the first time, I admired, as I should have, a number of beautiful things which he has in it. However, I do not understand how he conceives weight or attraction. It seems that, according to him, it is only a certain incorporeal and inexplicable virtue, while you explain it very plausibly through the laws of mechanics."

Huyghens, in his reply, showed his agreement with this judgment on Newton: "As for the cause of the reflux that Mr. Newton gives, I am not at all satisfied with it, nor with all the other theories which he builds on his principle of attraction, which appears absurd to me, as I have already testified in the Addition to the *Discours de la Pesanteur.* And I have often wondered how he could have taken the trouble to do so much research and so many difficult computations which have as their foundation only this same principle." However, somewhere else in his correspondence with Leibniz, he appears as a more coherent relativist than the latter: "I cannot agree with you that a number of bodies which are mutually in relative motion have a certain degree of motion or of veritable force." Unfortunately, Huyghens did not succeed in solving the Newtonian problem of absolute rotation.

6. Cartesianism from d'Alembert to Hertz

6.1. THE EIGHTEENTH CENTURY

Descartes wished to base physics entirely on mechanics, which he conceived as a pure geometry of motion.

Descartes' essential ideas are summarized in the two following excerpts from his works:

Concerning matter he asserts:

> In examining the nature of this matter, I find that it consists of nothing but its extension in length, width, and depth, so that everything that has three dimensions is a part of this matter; and there cannot be any entirely empty space, that is, containing no matter, because we cannot conceive of such a space without conceiving of it in these three dimensions and consequently matter (*Oeuvres,* vol. V, pp. 51–52, Letter to Chaunt, June 6, 1647).

As far as motion is concerned, he defines it as:

> The moving of a part of matter or of a body from the neighborhood of those that touch it and that we consider at rest, to the neighborhood of others (*Principia Philosophiae* II, XXV, French translation by l'Abbé Picot, reviewed by Descartes himself).

We must point out the Descartes' effective contribution to the development of mechanics is practically nil. In his famous polemic with Leibniz, it is clear that his idea of quantity of motion is erroneous to the extent that he conceived it as a scalar and not a vectoral dimension. That is why his deductions on the conduct of mechanical systems, particularly his famous seven rules on the

impact of elastic bodies, are false. Nevertheless, Mach himself, so
merciless in the criticism of his errors, gave him special credit:
"The merit of having first *sought after* a more universal and more
fruitful point of view in mechanics cannot be denied Descartes"
(Ernst Mach, *Science of Mechanics,* English translation by Thomas
J. McCormack. Open Court Publishing Co. La Salle, Ill. London,
1942, p. 364).

We can state positively that the whole eighteenth century, beginning wih Euler, the Bernoullis, and Clairault, and especially
through d'Alembert and Lagrange, was looking, in one way or another, for this "more general" point of view that would enable
them to get around the difficulties peculiar to the Newtonian
formulation.

D'Alembert occupies a very particular position in this list because of his explicit way of leaning toward the analysis of basic
concept. In his *Traité de Dynamique,* not only "the laws of equilibrium and of the motion of bodies are reduced to the smallest
number possible, and are demonstrated in a new way"—according to the subtitle of the book—but we also find in it "the examination of another important question, proposed by the Royal Acad-
emy of Sciences of Prussia, whether the laws of statics and mechanics are truly necessary or contingent."

In the *Discours Préliminaire* of this work, d'Alembert states
from the beginning that "the certainty of mathematics is an advantage that this science owes principally to the simplicity of its
object." Nevertheless, all parts of mathematics do not have the
same simplicity. In reality, "only those that deal with the computation of dimensions and with the general properties of extension,
that is, algebra, geometry, and mechanics, can be considered as
stamped with the seal of evidence." Now, the three are not on the
same plane. There is a gradation that goes from algebra to geometry and from the latter to mechanics, by increasing the complexity
of their object and, consequently, by diminishing their degree of
evidence. The reason for that must be sought—according to
d'Alembert—in the fact that "our ideas seem to become more
obscure the more we examine perceptible properties in an object."

It is precisely from this point of view, that is, from the relative
position of the sciences concerning the "certainty" that is peculiar

to them, that d'Alembert judged his work: "Fortunately, we have applied algebra to geometry, geometry to mechanics, and each of these three sciences to all the others whose basis and foundation they are."

For d'Alembert, motion and its general properties are the first and principal object of mechanics. But the existence of motion is "presupposed without any other particular hypothesis." The three principles with which he was going to try to find the solution to all the problems of motion are the principles of the force of inertia, of compound motion, and of equilibrium. The three were, for d'Alembert, necessary truths:

> We have shown that all laws of the communication of motion between bodies are reduced to laws of equilibrium, and that laws of equilibrium are themselves reduced to those of the equilibrium of two equal bodies activated in opposite directions with equal, virtual speeds. In this last case, the motions of the two bodies will evidently destroy each other, and, as a geometric consequence, there will necessarily still be an equilibrium when the masses are in inverse ratio to the speeds.

The concept of force enters into the mechanics of d'Alembert only as an impulse produced by impacts. The only definition of force used is of a kinematic type given by a relationship in the form of $ft = v$.

D'Alembert's program was distinctly Cartesian in style. But he departed from the Cartesians, whom, moreover, he treated disdainfully, on two fundamental points. The first referred to the identity of matter and extension.

D'Alembert rejected the idea of considering extension and matter as being the same thing. On the contrary, he considered two kinds of extension:

> One, which may be regarded as impenetrable and which constitutes what we properly call bodies; the other, which, being simply considered as extended without considering whether it is penetrable or not, may be the measure of the distance of one body to another the parts of which, viewed as fixed and immobile, might be used to determine the rest or the motion of bodies. It will, therefore,

always be possible for us to conceive of an indefinite space as the locus of bodies, whether real or supposed, and to consider motion as the transfer of the mobile from one place to another.

Even though the ideas expressed here are Newtonian, the process used to translate the laws of motion into equations is, as we have already indicated, clearly Cartesian.

The second divergence in respect to the Cartesians is the establishment of a fundamental difference between geometry and mechanics.

> Consideration of motion sometimes enters into the studies of pure geometry. [But,] geometry considers in motion only the space traveled, whereas in mechanics we are in addition concerned with the time that the mobile takes to cover this space.

This consideration of the role of time in mechanics was not to be completely understood, as we know, until the theory of relativity.

D'Alembert's line of thinking was continued by Lagrange in his *Mécanique analytique,* considered by science historians as "the work that summarizes and crowns the whole effort of the eighteenth century in the elaboration of a rationally organized mechanics" (R. Dugas, *Histoire de la mécanique*).

Lagrange thought that the principle of the lever and the principle of the composition of forces were sufficient to serve as a foundation for statics, but he was opposed to those who reduced the latter "to just a result of geometric constructions or of analysis."

> We must admit that by separating thus the principle of the composition of forces from that of the composition of motions, we cause it to lose its principal advantages, evidence and simplicity.

Nevertheless, he developed his statics on the basis of a single more general principle, the principle of virtual speeds, concerning which he stated:

> Whether we look upon the principle of virtual speeds as a general property of equilibrium, as Galileo did, or whether we wish to

consider it, along with Descartes and Wallis, as the true cause of equilibrium, we must admit that it has all the simplicity we could ask for in a fundamental principle.

It would seem that Lagrange carried on, to some extent, Leibniz's line of thinking, which is Duhem's opinion, for example, by placing the concept of force, as a fundamental notion, at the point of departure of his construction of mechanics. But this resemblance, which is only superficial, as we are about to see, leans on the fact that "analytical mechanics" begins with the definition of *"force* or *power"* as "the cause, whatever it may be, that transmits or tends to transmit motion to the body to which we presume it to be applied." Later Hertz pointed out that Lagrange "must certainly have perceived the logical difficulty of such a definition." However, Lagrange made no elaboration subsequent to this concept of force; on the contrary, he continued the procedure adopted by d'Alembert by expressing force as velocity divided by time.

Lagrange, as opposed to d'Alembert, made no analysis of fundamental concepts. His aim was to "reduce mechanics to purely analytic operations," and he achieved it with extraordinary parsimony and rigor. In doing so he manifested indirectly an implicit Cartesianism.

The notion of force appeared in Lagrange's equations as subsumed in a broadened concept: that of generalized force. In this way it lost its character as a fundamental concept irreducible to other concepts. The resulting structure, therefore, departed from the Leibnizian tradition.

6.2. HERTZ AND THE ELIMINATION OF FORCE

In his Introduction to his *Principles of Mechanics,* Hertz clearly summarized the foundations of what he called *the customary representation of mechanics.* The principal architects of this "representation" in its historical unfolding are—according to Hertz—Archimedes, Galileo, Newton, and Lagrange. The basic ideas are those of space, time, force, and mass. The idea of force is introduced as the cause of motion existing before motion itself and independent of it. The interconnections are explained in the following manner:

Space and force appear at first *by themselves,* and their relationships are considered in statics. Kinematics, or science of pure motion, is reduced to making the connection between the two ideas of space and time. Galileo's concept concerning inertia provides a connection between space, time, and mass, and nothing else. It is not until Newton's laws of motion that the four fundamental ideas could be connected to each other. These laws contain the germ of future developments, but they provide no general expression to express the influence of rigid spatial connections. D'Alembert's principle applies here the general results of statics to the case of motion, thus bringing to a close the series of independent fundamental statements that cannot be deduced one from the other. From here on, all is deductive inference.

Hertz subjected this method of founding mechanics to a thorough, critical examination, and he tried to reconstruct it on clearer foundations by reducing to a minimum the fundamental concepts. His *Principles of Mechanics*—his last work, written just before his death at the age of 37—elicited the admiration, if not the total acceptance, of two such severe critics as Mach and Boltzmann. "In the beautiful ideal form which Hertz has given to mechanics," says Mach (*Science of Mechanics,* p. 364), "its physical contents have shrunk to an apparently almost imperceptible residue. There is little doubt that if Descartes were alive today, he would have seen his own ideal in Hertz' mechanics far more than in Lagrange's analytical geometry of four dimensions."

Likewise, Boltzmann stated that: "The principles of mechanics established by Hertz are of an extraordinary simplicity and beauty. They are naturally not entirely free from being arbitrary, but I would willingly say that the arbitrariness is reduced to a minimum."

Given the characteristics of the reconstruction of mechanics brought about by Hertz, the two evaluations just quoted acquired great importance to the extent that they clearly showed how much a certain degree of arbitrariness was admitted to be inevitable by physicists working with the greatest intensity on the problems of the foundation of mechanics in the transition period between the nineteenth and twentieth centuries.

In his reconstruction of mechanics, Hertz used only the three fundamental and *independent* concepts of time, space, and mass considered as objects of experience. First of all, he looked for the connections between pairs of these ideas. The relationships between space and time constitute kinematics. There are no relationships that just connect mass and time. On the other hand, there are some between mass and space, and they are important. Certain positions and certain changes of position are prescribed as being possible for masses, completely independent of time, whereas all others are considered as impossible. These connections are applicable only to the positions of the masses relative to each other. They must be respected in the same way as certain conditions of continuity. On this basis Hertz constructed mechanics by combining the connections between the three fundamental notions into one law: "All natural motion of an independent material system consists of the fact that the system continues with a uniform velocity along the most rectilinear path possible." As Hertz himself indicated, this law condenses into one principle the principle of inertia and Gauss' principle of least constraint. He expressed it thus: "If the connections of the system were to be momentarily destroyed, its masses would disperse in a straight line and with a constant velocity; however, since this is impossible, they try to come as close as possible to such a movement." It is from this principle, and especially with the help provided by the analytical mechanics of Lagrange, that Hertz reconstructed mechanics.

This attempt to reconstruct the whole of mechanics on a single law of least constraint had two important consequences. First, the concept of force as a fundamental idea disappeared. It was replaced by that of connection between masses. Second, Hertz was forced to make a dangerous supposition: "As far as masses are concerned, we shall establish that, in addition to masses that can be recognized through the senses, hidden masses can be introduced by hypothesis." The replacement of forces by "connections" required the supposition that, when the connections are not visible, there are hidden masses activated by hidden movements. This somewhat surprising idea was, nevertheless, no less acceptable nor less troubling than the actions at a distance admitted in Newtonian mechanics. If Hertz' ideas found no adherents or anyone to carry them on, it was not because they were rejected for theoretical reasons. "The model constructed by Hertz independent of experience," Boltzmann stresses, "possesses a perfection and an evidence that are both definite; it contains only a few arbitrary elements." But such a mechanics was difficult to conceive in its practical applications. Boltzmann's definitive judgment was this:

> Consequently Hertz' mechanics appears to me rather as a program for the distant future. Once we have succeeded in explaining all the processes of nature by hidden movements, in the Hertzian sense, and doing it in a way that is not too artificial, the old mechanics will yield to that of Hertz. Until then, classical mechanics appears as the only one capable of clearly explaining phenomena, without bothering to look for objects that are not only hidden, but that we cannot even begin to imagine.

The value of Hertz' work thus remains only academic, but it can be considered a result of the type of speculation characteristic of the seventeenth century. Hertz, at the end of the nineteenth century, thus closed the cycle begun with Galileo, Descartes, Newton, and Huyghens. After a century and a half of efforts, the construction remained unfinished. The twentieth century found better solutions, but not before delving still more deeply into the foundations and submitting to critical analysis not only the ideas of mass and of force, but also and especially, the concepts of space and time. This work was Einstein's, who picked up again, probably without realizing it, the line of thinking that had begun with Leibniz.

7. *The Renaissance of Leibnizian Ideas*

In his famous lecture in 1854—published posthumously by Dedekind in 1867—Riemann introduced a revolutionary idea on the relationships between geometry and physics. Riemann generalized the theory developed by Gauss concerning the concept of the curvature of a surface by applying it to the manifold of an arbitrary number of dimensions. He thus arrived at the idea—which Einstein later took up—of an unlimited but finite space:

When the constructions of space are extended to the immeasurably great, the distinction must be made between the unlimited and the infinite, the first one belonging to the relationships of extension, the second to metric relationships. That space is an unlimited three-dimensional manifold is a hypothesis that is applied to all our concepts of the external world, which we constantly use to complete the realm of our actual perceptions and to construct the possible positions of a sought-for object, and which is constantly being verified in all these applications. The limitlessness of space, therefore, possesses a much greater empirical certainty than any other external experience. However, infinity in no way follows; rather, if we presuppose that bodies are independent of positions and that we thus attribute to space a rate of constant curvature, space would necessarily be finite, since this rate of curvature has a positive value, however small it may be. By prolonging along shorter lines the initial directions in a superficial element, we would obtain an unlimited surface as a measure of constant curvature, that is, a surface which in a three-dimensional plane manifold would take the shape of a spherical surface and which would consequently be finite.

The central notion used here is that of the subordination of the properties of space to the properties of matter. The most important paragraph of Riemann's exposé establishes that:

The question of the validity of the hypotheses of geometry in the infinitely small is linked with the question of the intimate principles of the metric relationships in space. In this last question, which we can still regard as belonging to the doctrine of space, the above remark can be applied, namely, that in a discrete manifold the principle of metric relationships is already contained in the concept of this manifold, while in a constant manifold this principle must come from somewhere else. It is necessary, therefore, either that the reality on which space is founded form a discrete manifold or that the foundation of the metric relationships be looked for outside it, in the connecting forces that act on it.

The clearest interpretation of Riemann's ideas was made by H. Weyl in his book *Space, Time, Matter* [translated from the German by Henry L. Brose].

. . . we see that Riemann rejects the opinion that had pre-
vailed up to his own time, namely, that the metrical structure of
space is fixed and inherently independent of the physical phenomena
for which it serves as a background, and that the real content
takes possession of it as of residential flats. He asserts, on the
contrary, that space in itself is nothing more than a three-dimensional manifold devoid of all form; it acquires a definite form
only through the advent of the material content filling it and
determining its metric relations.

Einstein went even further than Riemann. According to his
general theory of relativity, an empty space, that is, a space without a field, does not exist. If the gravitational field is eliminated,
there remains "absolutely *nothing,* not even a topological space,"
because the functions that describe the gravitational field "describe not only the field, but also simultaneously the topological
and metrical structural properties of the manifold." [1]

The elimination of the notion of space from the foundation of
mechanics had already been proposed by Mach toward the end
of the nineteenth century. Mach criticized Descartes' concept, according to which all physics was based on mechanics conceived
as a pure geometry of motion. Descartes did not have a clear idea
of mass and, consequently, he did not take into consideration the
fact that "mechanics is possible only on the condition that the
positions of the bodies are determined, in their dependence on
one another, by a relation of forces by a function of time" (Mach,
ibid., p. 369).

According to Mach, completely empty space has no structure.
The geometric properties of space are determined exclusively by
the matter that occupies it. To a certain extent, we can say that
there is here a reformulation of Leibniz's and Riemann's positions.
But Mach pushes the analysis a little further, and again questions
the concept of inertia as it appears in Newton's laws. "When,
accordingly, we say that a body preserves unchanged its direction and velocity in *space,* our assertion is nothing more or less

---

[1] A. Einstein, *La relativité et le problème de l'espace,* Paris, Gauthier-
Villars, 1956.

than an abbreviated reference to *the entire universe*" (Mach, *ibid.,*
p. 286). The motion of a body K is not *related to space*. Instead,
we make the direct study of the relationships of K with all the
bodies of the universe. Thus, "instead of saying that the direction
and velocity of a mass μ in space remains constant, we may also
employ the expression, the mean acceleration of the mass μ with
respect to the masses m, m', m'', . . . at the distances r, r', r'',
. . . is zero, or $d^2(\epsilon\, mr/\epsilon\, m)/d \pm {}^2 = 0$. The latter expression is
equivalent to the former as soon as we take into consideration a
sufficient number of sufficiently distant and sufficiently large
masses. The mutual influence of more proximate small masses,
which are apparently not concerned about each other, is eliminated
of itself" (Mach, *ibid.,* p. 286).

Mach's central idea is that *all* masses are in mutual relationships. Even in the simplest case, in which apparently we deal
only with the mutual action between two masses, it is impossible
to disregard the rest of the universe. Thus Mach answered Clarke's
last question, left unanswered by the death of Leibniz. There is
no *absolute* rotation. In the experiment of the pail filled with
water and set in motion by a rotating movement, the apparent
centrifugal forces "are awakened" by the relative movement of
the water "in relation to the mass of the earth and to the other
celestial bodies." According to Mach:

> There exists, in short, only a relative movement, and in this
> respect I perceive *no* distinction between rotation and translation.
> A rotation in relation to *fixed stars* gives birth in a body to forces
> that pull it away from the axis; if the rotation is not relative to the
> fixed stars, these repelling forces do not exist. I am not opposed
> to giving to the first rotation the term *absolute,* provided that we
> do not forget that it is nothing more than a *relative* rotation in rela-
> tion *to the fixed stars.* Can we fasten down Newton's water bucket,
> can we then make the sky of the fixed stars turn, and *then prove*
> that these repelling forces are absent? This experiment is un-
> realizable, this idea is deprived of meaning because the *two* cases
> are indistinguishable one from the other in sensory perception. I
> therefore consider these *two* cases as forming only *one* and the
> distinction that Newton makes as illusory (Mach, *La Mécanique,*
> French translation, p. 231).

A direct consequence of this point of view is that there is no essential difference between gravity and inertia. The same mechanical forces are interpreted as gravity or as inertia, according to the system of coordinates chosen as a reference. Consequently, and contrary to what Newton maintained, there is no type of inertial force that can be taken as an indication of an absolute motion.

Thus Mach appears as the first relativist (in spite of himself, since he declared himself as antirelativistic in his posthumous work, *Les Principes de l'optique physique*). Einstein often refers to what he calls "Mach's principle," that is, to the dependency of inertia (translational and rotational) on distribution on a large scale and on the movement of matter.

8. The Concept of Geometry in the Theory of Relativity

8.1. The axiomatization of Euclidean geometry and the development of non-Euclidean geometries have constituted decisive milestones in the process of the progressive enlightenment of the old problem of the relationships between geometry and the physical world. Probably the best synthesis of the problem was made by Einstein himself: "How is it possible that mathematics, which is the product of human thought and independent of all experience, can adapt itself so admirably to the objects of reality?" And he continues: "In my opinion it is necessary to answer this question in the following way: To the extent that mathematical propositions relate to reality, they are not certain; and to the extent that they are certain, they do not relate to reality" (Einstein, *Geometry and Experience*).

In this famous statement by Einstein, the distinction between mathematical geometry and physical geometry is clearly expressed. It is physical geometry, that is, the geometry of physical space, that remains a problem. In this respect the theory of relativity constituted the most profound revision of its foundations in the whole history under consideration here.

This revision was made in two steps, corresponding, successively, to the field of special relativity and to that of general relativity.

8.2. In the Introduction to the memorandum in which he presented for the first time his theory of special relativity (*On the Electrodynamics of Moving Bodies*), Einstein starts with "the supposition that not only in mechanics, but also in electrodynamics, no properties of observed facts correspond to a concept of absolute rest; but that for all coordinate systems for which the mechanical equations hold, the equivalent electrodynamical and optical equations hold also, as has already been shown for magnitudes of the first order."

Einstein introduced this supposition, which he was about to raise "to the rank of a hypothesis," starting with the asymmetries of Maxwell's electrodynamics applied to moving bodies, and with the negative results of the famous experiment of Michelson and Morley to show the movement of the earth in relation to "the environment in which light is propagated."

By thus applying to electromagnetic phenomena the concept of relativity that is valid in Newtonian physics for mechanical phenomena, Einstein immediately introduced a methodological revolution. He translated the experimental results into a fundamental principle and, starting from this point, he reformulated the concepts on which classical physics was constructed. The same line of thinking led him to introduce another supposition (which was really only a corollary of the previous one when the latter was applied to Maxwell's equations): "Light is propagated in a vacant space with a velocity c that is independent of the nature of motion of the emitting body." On this base Einstein constructed an electrodynamics of moving bodies "simple and free from contradictions."

The last paragraph of the Introduction of the memorandum already mentioned is of particular interest for the subject we are considering here:

> Like every other theory in electrodynamics, the theory is based on the kinematics of rigid bodies; in the enunciation of every theory, we have to do with relations between rigid bodies (coordinate system), clocks, and electromagnetic processes. An in-

sufficient consideration of these circumstances is the cause of difficulties with which the electrodynamics of moving bodies have to fight at present.

It is precisely the analysis of the function carried out by rigid bodies and clocks that constituted the beginning of the Einsteinian revolution in the fundamental concepts of physics.

8.3. It is not the aim of this work to develop the principles of the theory of relativity, nor to establish the precise differences between the special theory of relativity and the general theory of relativity. A brief review of a few fundamental facts will suffice.

In special relativity, space and time no longer have completely independent roles: They are replaced by the concept of a four-dimensional manifold. A point in this manifold represents an event determined by three spatial coordinates and a temporal coordinate. Thus two point events in an inertial reference frame determine an interval that can be expressed in Cartesian coordinates by Minkowski's relationship:

$$ds^2 = c^2\,dt^2 - dx^2 - dy^2 - dz^2 \qquad (1)$$

(c = speed of light).

This fact was expressed by Minkowski in the famous statement: "Henceforth, space as such and time as such are doomed to fade away into mere shadows, and only a kind of union of the two will preserve an independent reality."

Nevertheless, the statement is not entirely correct. The fact of considering time as a fourth coordinate that is added to the three spatial dimensions in order to determine a four-dimensional spacetime adds no particular characteristic to time. In reality, this procedure is perfectly valid in prerelativistic classical mechanics.

The relationship between space and time introduced by relativity has a more profound meaning than the relationship itself. It can be summarized in the three following statements:

(a) There are two fundamental procedures for measuring time intervals: counting periodic events, and measuring distances (spatial) in the case of nonperiodic processes. In both cases we associate a time interval with a certain type of process, which entails certain suppositions about physical mechanisms that regulate these processes.

(b) There is no way to determine empirically the equality of two *consecutive* time intervals. The laws that lead to the establishment of the isochronism of the oscillations of a pendulum, for example, implicitly contain the supposition of the equality of consecutive time intervals in a certain basic system. Any "demonstration" or "verification" is therefore circular.

(c) The comparison of periods of time during which two events occur at a distance from each other in space, in particular the definition of the simultaneity of two distant events, is still based on the transmission of signals from one point to another in space. This presupposes a knowledge of the distance and of the speed of the signal. The identification of light as a signal that is propagated faster than any other and that possesses, in addition, a finite speed, requires the introduction of definitions with a certain degree of arbitrariness in relation to speeds—for example, the supposition that the speed of propagation in two opposite directions is the same. These definitions include, in turn, a definition of equally arbitrary simultaneity. The definition of simultaneity is thus deprived of absolute meaning.

(d) The intimate link between the concepts of space and time becomes manifest as soon as we consider the difficulties encountered when we try to go from the definition of the length of a segment of a straight line "at rest" to the definition of the length of a segment moving at a given velocity. In one way or another we arrive at a definition of the type: "The length of a segment of a moving straight line is the distance between the *simultaneous* positions of its initial and final points." Measurements of space, therefore, depend on the definition of simultaneity.

It is this reciprocal dependence between the fundamental concepts used to define spatial relationships, on the one hand, and temporal relationships, on the other, when events occur at a distance from each other, that gives its true meaning to Minkowski's proposition. Nevertheless, for each observer, the spatial coordinates and the temporal coordinate preserve an immediate physical meaning. In Minkowski's universe there are still spacelike intervals and timelike intervals.

8.4. The principle of relativity, according to which all inertial systems are equivalent in regard both to mechanical and electromagnetic phenomena, gives to inertial frames of reference a privileged position. Physical laws acquire their simplest formulations when motion is referred to such frames. They constitute, in addition, standards for determining acceleration.

Mach, in his critique of Newton's idea of absolute acceleration, had been led, as we indicated in § 4, to identify inertia with gravitational effects; but gravitation itself remained as incomprehensible as it was in Newton's formulation, to the extent that Mach still had to postulate action at a distance. Einstein kept the central idea of Mach's formulation, which he called "Mach's principle," but he inverted, so to speak, the terms of the relationship. Gravitation was explained to a certain extent by inertia and not the reverse. Inertia became, then, a problem for the general theory of relativity. Einstein's point of departure is the *principle of equivalence,* which he introduced with his famous example of the elevator cut loose from its point of suspension and dropping in free fall to the ground. Newton's laws, applied to experiments inside the elevator (considered as a laboratory), show that all mechanical phenomena take place as if the elevator were an inertial system. Einstein postulated this equivalence as valid for all physical phenomena. Therefore, a laboratory in "free fall" toward a mass with a powerful gravitational field acts in the same way as a laboratory away from the attraction of any mass and immobile in relation to the "fixed stars."

According to Newton, gravitational force can be measured in terms of the coordinates of an inertial reference frame. The gravitational effects, therefore, are added to the inertial frame.

According to the principle of equivalence, a gravitational field can be transformed in such a way that it disappears as such and remains only as an effect of inertia. Any event can thus be associated with an inertial system of coordinates. Nevertheless, such a system has only a local validity, namely, that in the neighborhood of the event in question, an interval *ds* is determined by Minkowski's expression. But this inertial frame cannot be extended indefinitely into space. In Einstein's theory there are no inertial frames other than these local ones. There is no privileged frame in relation to which we can determine the gravitational field. The field is different for moving reference frames. Relativism is not total. There is an invariant that expresses the state of the universe when it comes to the reciprocal action of its masses. This invariant is apparent from the fact that each system of coordinates conjointly with its gravitational field, that is, the field, expressed in terms of these coordinates, is equivalent to any other system of coordinates with its corresponding gravitational field.

Mathematically, this means that the gravitational field can be represented by a tensor whose components change with the system of coordinates. But the tensor itself is an invariant. This tensor coincides with the tensor that defines the metric of space.[1]

The g_{ik}'s, therefore, combine the effects of gravity and of inertia.

---

[1] For those who are not familiar with tensor calculus, we should introduce here some definitions.

A Riemannian space is a manifold in which the "distance" or the "interval" between two neighboring points $(x_1, x_2, \ldots, x_n)$ and $(x_1 + dx_1, x_2 + dx_2, \ldots, x_n + dx_n)$ is defined by the expression

$$ds^2 = g_{ik} \, dx_i \, dx_k \qquad (2)$$

The g_{ik}'s are functions of the coordinates. The expression that defines the value of the interval ds is called the metric of space. This expression constitutes a generalization of the Pythagorean theorem. Given ds as a scalar, its value must be independent of the system of coordinates; that is,

$$ds^2 = g_{ik} \, dx_i \, dx_k = g'_{ik} \, dx'_i \, dx'_k$$

From here on we can easily show that the g_{ik}'s are the components of a covariant tensor of the second rank.

The above considerations about the relationships between the gravitational field and the inertial systems, in the theory of relativity, can be expressed in the following way. In an inertial coordinate system (Galilean), the metric is given by Minkowski's relationship (1):

$$ds^2 = -dx^2 - dy^2 - dz^2 + c^2 \, dt^2$$

which is a particular case of the form (2), in which

$$x_1 = x; \quad x_2 = y; \quad x_3 = z; \quad x_4 = ct$$

and the g_{ik}'s are reduced to the Galilean form:

$$g_{11} = g_{22} = g_{33} = 1; \quad g_{44} = -1; \quad g_{ik} = 0 \quad \text{for } i \neq k \qquad (3)$$

In the presence of a gravitational field, the g_{ik}'s can always be reduced, in an infinitely small region of space and for an infinitely short interval of time, to the Galilean form, by means of an appropriate transformation of coordinates (that is, by means of the utilization of an inertial "local" reference frame). But there is no transformation that allows the g_{ik}'s to be reduced to the Galilean form (3) in all space. In other words, in the presence of gravitational fields, space-time is "locally plane," but it is "curved" beyond the neighborhood of the point considered. Gravitational fields are equivalent to noninertial systems and, consequently, they are determined by the metric tensor.

Action at a distance disappears. The motion of a planet is not determined by the force of attraction, exercised across empty space, by the sun and the other planets, but by the state of the metric field in the immediate neighborhood of the planet. Thus space acquires a function that goes further than the role of "environment" through which the forces are propagated or the "field" acts. Space is the field itself, and its configuration determines the possible motion of bodies.

The metric field changes when the position of bodies is modified. This change is not instantaneous. It is a question of an effect that is propagated from one point to another in space with a finite velocity: the speed of light. There is, therefore, a relationship between "the state of the metric field" and the distribution of masses. The general theory of relativity culminates with this relationship, the nature of which it is important to make explicit in terms of the perspective adopted here. With this in mind, we shall take as a point of departure Maxwell's electromagnetic theory reinterpreted from the point of view of the theory of relativity.

8.5. The method used by Maxwell in his *Treatise on Electricity and Magnetism* continues Lagrange's line of thinking. The laws that govern electromagnetic phenomena must be expressed by equations "that make their analogy to certain equations of motion very striking." But we make no hypothesis concerning the nature of this motion. To the extent that the phenomena can be translated by means of Lagrange's equations, the dimensions that characterize the system can be put into correspondence with the variables and the velocities that set the configuration and the motion of a certain mechanical system.

In electromagnetic theory, each charged particle creates an electromagnetic field, the properties of which are characterized by a four-vector A_i (functions of the coordinates of space and time) called electromagnetic potential. When a charged particle moves in the field, it is influenced by this field and, in turn, its motion modifies the field itself.

The motion of a particle with a charge e sufficiently small so that its displacement does not influence the field can be easily described starting with the principle of least action.[2] The "action"

---

[2] We are following here Landau and Lifschitz' method.

of the particle is constituted by two terms. The first term corresponds to the action of the particle considered as "free," that is, in the absence of a field. This action is

$$S_m = -mc \int_a^b ds; \quad (ds = \sqrt{-dx_i^2})$$

The second term corresponds to the interaction of the particle with the field. If we represent by A_t the potential of the field at time t at the point where the particle of charge e is located, the action is

$$S_{mf} = \frac{e}{c} \int_a^b A_t \, dx_t$$

The principle of least action establishes that

$$\delta S = \delta(S_m + S_{mf}) = 0$$

In the most general case of a system composed of an electromagnetic field and of particles that are found in it, the action can be considered as being made up of three parts: (a) the action due to the particles considered as free; (b) the action due to the interaction of particles with the field; (c) the action of the field in the absence of charges. To find the equations of motion of the particles, the field is supposedly known, and therefore we omit (c). To find the equations of the field, the motion of the charges is supposedly known and we only vary the potentials of the field.

Thus we arrive at Maxwell's equations:

$$\frac{\partial F_{ik}}{\partial x_l} + \frac{\partial F_{cl}}{\partial x_k} + \frac{\partial F_{kl}}{\partial x_l} = 0$$

$$(-g)^{-1/2} / \frac{\partial}{\partial x_k} [(-g)^{1/2} F^{ik}] = 0$$

where $g = g_{ik}$, and F_{ik} is called the electromagnetic field tensor. The covariant components are

$$F_{ik} = \frac{\partial A_k}{\partial x_i} \quad \frac{\partial A_t}{\partial x_k}$$

where F^{ik} are the contravariant components of the same tensor.

The spatial components of the tensor F_{ik} (those defined by $i, k = 1, 2, 3$) are related to those of the magnetic field; the temporal components (those defined by $i = 4$ or $k = 4$) are the components of the electrical field.

Starting with the principle of least action that led to the equations of motion, we can also define as a tensor the vector P_i, having for components the integrals of the T_{ik}'s:

$$P_i = -\lambda \int T_{ik}\, dS_k$$

coincides with the four-vector momentum of the system (dS_k is an element of the hypersurface containing all space in three dimensions). The tensor T_{ik} is the energy-momentum tensor of the system.

We can show that, in the case of an electromagnetic field without sources, Maxwell's equations let us express the energy-momentum tensor as a function of the electromagnetic field tensor and of the metric tensor:

$$T_{ik} = \frac{1}{4\pi}(F_{il}\, F_{kl} - \frac{1}{4}\, F^2_{\ lm}\ \delta_{ik})$$

One can then follow a path parallel to the one that led to Maxwell's equations and arrive, likewise starting from an action integral, at the equation of Einstein's gravitational field. (This procedure, which, however, was not the one originally followed by Einstein, offers a great simplicity and gives a great unity to the development of the theory. Cf., for example, Landau and Lifschitz, *Classical Theory of Fields.*)

The only difference is that the gravitational field is considered here as the modification of the metric of space-time, that is, the modification of ds in terms of the dx_i's. By the principle of least action,

$$\delta S = mc\, \delta \int ds = 0$$

This means that a particle moves in a gravitational field in such a manner that it describes a geodesic. The equation of motion is therefore arrived at by calculating the integral of

$$\delta(ds) = \delta(g_{ik}\, dx_i\, dx_k)$$

The energy-momentum tensor T_{ik} of macroscopic bodies is, moreover, defined by considering that the momentum flux through a surface element of a body is the force acting on this element.

The principle of least action applied to the gravitational field thus leads directly to Einstein's equations:

$$R_{ik} - \frac{1}{2}\, g_{ik} R = \frac{\chi}{c^2}\, T_{ik}$$

where χ is Einstein's gravitational constant; R is an invariant called the curvature scalar; R_{ik} is Ricci's tensor defined in terms of the g_{ik}'s and their derivatives exclusively; and T_{ik} is the energy-momentum tensor that represents both gravitational as well as electromagnetic phenomena.

These equations of the gravitational field constitute a surprising amalgam of geometry and physics. But before analyzing their meaning, we shall present the last step taken in this direction by the physics of relativity.

9. The Theoretical Foundations of the Complete Geometrization of the Physics of Relativity

The rise of geometrodynamics, beginning with the works of Misner and Wheeler, brought up a rather odd fact in the history of physics. Immediately after having formulated the general theory of relativity, Einstein tried to construct a "unified theory" capable of combining the laws of electromagnetism and gravity in a single system. His efforts continued throughout his life. His aim was to take into account all the results of quantum mechanics starting with a unified field theory. "When Einstein died (in 1956), his goal seemed as distant as ever," according to Born in his book, *Einstein's Theory of Relativity*. However, by 1925, G. Y. Rainich, in an article entitled "Electrodynamics in the General Relativity Theory" (published in the *Transactions of the American Mathematical Society*), had succeeded in combining into the same system of equations Maxwell's equations and Einstein's gravitational equations, thus showing that, under certain very general conditions, the electromagnetic field is entirely determined by the curvature of space-time. This article was ignored until it was rediscovered by Charles Misner after he arrived independently, in 1956, at the same results.

There are three surprising facts in this history. The first is that for more than 30 years, no one, not even Einstein, had noticed Rainich's results. The second is the simplicity of the method used by Rainich and Misner, and the fact that the unified field equations can be obtained "without adding anything" to Maxwell's and Einstein's equations (from then on the term "already unified theory" used by Misner and by Wheeler). The third is the fact that this "unified theory" hindered sufficient progress in the direction of the explanation of the results of quantum mechanics.

The procedure can be briefly described in the following manner. Maxwell's equations presented in the preceding sections,

$$\frac{\partial F_{ik}}{\partial x^l} + \frac{\partial F_{li}}{\partial x^k} + \frac{\partial F_{kl}}{\partial x^i} = 0$$

$$(-g)^{-1/2}\frac{\partial}{\partial x^k}[(-g)^{-1/2}F^{ik}] = 0$$

describe the electromagnetic field in terms of the fields themselves. The energy-momentum tensor T_{ik} is then calculated starting with the fields by means of the relationship we have already presented, which is, in curvilinear coordinates, of the form

$$T_{ik} = \frac{1}{4\pi}(F_{il}F_k{}^l - \frac{1}{4}g_{ik}F_{lm}F^{lm})$$

This energy-momentum tensor is linked to the metric of the universe by the equations of the gravitational field or Einstein's equations:

$$G_{ik} \equiv R_{ik} - \frac{1}{2}g_{ik}R = \frac{\chi}{c^2}T_{ik}$$

where χ is Einstein's gravitational constant.

Geometrodynamics reverses the direction of the process; the field equations are written in terms of the energy-momentum tensor and then the fields are derived from the tensor. Mathematically, the problem is resolved by expressing the components of the tensor F in terms of the G_{ik}'s, starting with the last two relationships, and by substituting the values thus obtained in the first two relationships. Rainich and Misner were successful in this program, easily formulated but mathematically complex in its effective realization. The result is expressed in a system of equations that can be written as

$$\frac{\partial a_i}{\partial x^k} - \frac{\partial a_k}{\partial x^i} = 0$$

where the a's are defined exclusively in terms of the G_{ik}'s.

To the extent that the definitions of R_{ik} and R are in terms of the metric tensor *g*, of components g_{ik}'s, it follows that this last system of equations, which links together the a's, contains only properties of Einsteinian space-time. We thus arrive at a purely geometric description: The equations are entirely geometric and they describe physical situations in which there can be gravitational as well as electromagnetic fields. According to Misner and Wheeler, these surprising results provide considerable support for a point of view expressed as follows: "There is nothing in the world except empty curved space. Matter, charge, electromagnetism, and other fields are only manifestations of the curvature of space," *Physics is geometry* ["Classical Physics as Geometry," *Annals of Physics*, 2 (1957), p. 526].

More precisely, the results show that: (a) the gravitational field at a point is nothing more than another number given to the curvature of space-time at this point ("mass deprived of mass"!); (b) the electromagnetic field at a point is determined by the variation of this curvature in the neighborhood of this point ("electromagnetic field deprived of electromagnetic field"!). We must specify, even if we are not going to dwell on it, that the curved space we are talking about is not topologically equivalent to Euclidean space. In this theory the so-called electric charges are only manifestations of multiply connected regions of space.

However, it is necessary to take into account the fact that all these results apply only to classical and relativistic physics. For quantum mechanics, the situation is more complex, and the progress almost nonexistent (despite certain interesting results obtained by Wheeler). Besides, we do not know how to tackle the problem, because it does not seem possible to obtain Rainich's and Misner's equations starting with a variational principle as in the case of Einstein's and Maxwell's equations, according to the method sketched in the preceding section. This imposes limitations on the application of the theory to atomic physics. Dirac has clearly shown that, when we succeed in formulating a clasical theory starting with Hamilton's principle of action, it is then possible to apply certain standard rules to obtain a first approximation to a quantum theory (*Lectures on Quantum Mechanics*, Belfer Graduate School of Science, Yeshiva University, New York, 1964). In addition: "In reality, without making use of Hamilton's methods we cannot resolve some of the simplest problems in quantum theory" (*ibid.*, p. 3).

Apart from the difficulties that we find again when we try to quantize geometrodynamics, we want to emphasize here that the reduction of relativistic physics to a geometry of empty curved space poses problems of great interest from the epistemological point of view. We shall concern ourselves with them in the following section.

10. Analysis or Synthesis?

The equations of gravity in the general theory of relativity constitute the apex of Riemann's ideas already cited: "Therefore, either the reality on which space is founded must form a unique entity, or we must look for the foundation of metric relations outside of it, in the connective forces that act on it." Einstein succeeds in bringing about this amalgam of geometry and physics, of which Leibniz already had an intuition. By writing these equations in the form

$$G_{ik} \equiv R_{ik} - \frac{1}{2} g_{ik} R = \frac{\chi}{c^2} T_{ik}$$

the tensor T_{ik}, the energy-momentum tensor, acts as a source of a gravitational field. But R_{ik} as well as R contain only the metric tensor g and its derivatives. Consequently, the G_{ik}'s constitute purely geometric entities. The ten quantities g, therefore, represent at the same time the metric field and the gravitational field, which are only different aspects of the same thing.

Nevertheless, these equations have been diversely interpreted since their formulation by Einstein in 1916. At the outset, they were interpreted as constituting a triumph of Cartesianism, that is, as a breakdown of mechanics into geometry. Weyl, for example, thought that they modified "the old conception" of physics, which could be expressed thus:

> The four-dimensional metrical continuum is the theater of physical phenomena; the physical entities themselves are precisely

those that exist in this universe, and we must accept them in type and number in the form in which experience gives us cognition of them (*op. cit.*, p. 284).

The new conception leads, according to Weyl, to the following consequences:

The universe is a (3 + 1)-dimensional metrical manifold: all physical phenomena are expressions of its metric (*op. cit.*, p. 283).

And he adds:

Descartes' dream of a purely geometric physics seems to be attaining fulfillment in a manner that is entirely natural yet unforseen (*op. cit.*, p. 284).

Despite Weyl's authority, it would seem more coherent to interpret the equations in another way: It is not that the theory of gravity was geometrized, it is that geometry became the expression of the gravitational field. With this interpretation geometry is finally established on a solid basis. Not only can the geometry of the universe be established empirically, but in addition, it can be explained by the single effect of forces. A typical defender of this position is Reichenbach (*The Philosophy of Space and Time,* pp. 256–257). He agrees that the combination of the motion of planets with the motion of a free particle in one and the same law, which establishes motion of the whole length of a geodesic, suggests a purely geometric concept of gravity. But, he adds, the changes in the metric field are due to changes in the distribution of matter, which are propagated at the speed of light. Not only is the metric field determined by "a real physical process of causal propagation" but, in addition, "the effect of the metric field on the planet can be interpreted as a real physical force that guides it in its path."

This concept of the Einsteinian theory clearly constitutes the extreme consequence of Leibniz's ideas. There is neither space nor time independent of matter; there is no "action at a distance" across empty space. There are only matter and forces that act on it. All the rest, space and time included, is only a consequence.

Paradoxically, this "physicalization" of geometry was debated anew when geometrodynamics brought about the unification of the gravitational and electromagnetic fields into a single system of equations. Indeed, the "already unified" general theory of relativity ended up in a system of equations in which appeared only relationships between variables designating geometric entities. These equations were obtained through elimination of variables designating "physical" entities between Maxwell's equations of the electromagnetic field and Einstein's equations of the gravitational field. This detour *through* relationships that are not by nature purely geometric seemed inevitable. But before analyzing this problem, let us consider some of the immediate consequences of the theory:

(a) To the extent that the equations of dynamics are transformed into equations that relate only geometric entities, the only dimension that remains is length. Measures of weight (or of mass), expressed in grams, for example, are only suitable abbreviations of relationships between lengths expressed in centimeters.

(b) There are no longer "physical constants." The speed of light, for example, is only a number that expresses relationships between different units of length, *just as 5280 is the factor of conversion between miles and feet.*

(c) Electrical charges are not foreign entities that exist *in* space, but are characteristics *of* space. In reality, they are only a manifestation of multiply connected regions of space.

(d) Objects are names attributed to localizations of certain types of curvature in empty space.

Could we think of a Cartesianism more absolute than that expressed by these four propositions?

However, this does not imply that physics—or even classical and relativistic mechanics—is "quite simply" a geometry. In this *empty* curved space there are still motions and interactions subject to laws that must be postulated *in addition* to the postulates of geometry, and that are subject to experimental confirmation (or invalidation).

In this empty curved space there are still "physical phenomena." Where, then, is the link between the "purely geometric" equations of the "unified theory" and these "physical phenomena"? The answer must be sought precisely in the definition of the "geometric" concepts that intervene in the equations, in particular, in the nature of the g's that express the metric of space. The fundamental relationship $ds^2 = g_{ik} \, dx_i \, dx_k$ determines the value of the interval s in space-time. In the definition of g, the elements of the matrix that correspond to the variable "time" cannot be replaced by the others.

Minkowski's notion of "interval" in space-time, used by the special theory of relativity and defined by the quadratic form ds^2, embraces a distinction between "timelike intervals" and "spacelike intervals" that has an absolute character. An interval is either a timelike interval or a spacelike interval entirely independent of the reference frame. The "fusion" of space and time in the special theory of relativity is not, therefore, complete. Mathematically, the distinction is clear, since a timelike interval is represented by a real number, whereas a spacelike interval is represented by an imaginary one. The general theory of relativity uses a Riemannian space-time that is "locally" identical to Minkowski's space-time. This means simply that all Riemannian space is a Euclidean space in an infinitesimal region. Space and time appear integrated in the representation of Minkowski's space-time (Euclidean) only to the extent that, beyond an area of "absolute future" and one of "absolute past," there are areas, in relation to a "point" (spatiotemporal), in which the past and the future are indeterminate. But *there is* an "absolute" future. His definition is linked to nothing other than the propagation of signals and the existence of a maximum speed of propagation. At the very heart of spatiotemporal "metrics" we find, therefore, physical events, signals that are propagated and a succession of events identified as belonging to a causal chain. If relativistic physics can be reduced to relationships in which only the metric tensor of four-dimensional space intervenes, it is equally true that this tensor is stripped of all meaning outside a world in which there are physical events and causal chains.

Having arrived at this point, it is difficult to say whether we have brought about a complete geometrization of mechanics, or the reverse. Apparently, it is a question of a convergence of concepts toward a common synthesis, rather than a process of breaking down one discipline into another. In the final analysis, there remains only a "field," the different parts of which interact and undergo mutual displacements. Whether we call such a field "geometric" or "physical" seems to be an arbitrary decision. The fact that the parameters that intervene in the "unified" equations are considered as geometric elements results much more from an historical tradition than from a statement based on a distinction that can be made without falling into a vicious circle. Only genetic studies on the origin of notions that play a role in the basic equations could give this distinction the necessary basis.

Index